LIBRARY AND INFORMATION SCIENCE

CONCEPTS IN COMMUNICATION INFORMATICS & LIBRARIANSHIP (CICIL)

For a list of titles in this series
please see pp. 196 at the end of the book

About the Author

SISTER M. ESPERANZA, A.C., is the author of two other publications namely, *Public and Academic Libraries* in 1991 and *Perspectives of Library Movement in India* in 1994. She has also co-edited the Volume on *Dimensions of Library & Information Science - Kaula Festchrift* in 1990. Sister Esperanza qualified herself in B.Lib. Information Science from Patna University, securing 1st Division with First Rank.

She has contributed richly of her knowledge on various aspects of Library Management and Organisation as well as of other library activities at several conferences organized by I.L.A., AIACHE and IASLIC, held at Mysore, Madras, Bangalore, Jaipur, Delhi, Benaras, Trichur, Trivandrum, Lucknow, Patna and other places in India. The papers presented are published in the respective Seminar Volumes.

The authoress has also organized Workshops, Library Orientation Programmes, Book Exhibitions, Symposia and Talks on the use of library to conscientize the various types of readers and users of libraries for a better use of library materials and to encourage reading habits among them. Besides, several talks have been delivered by the authoress on practical managerial and organizational techniques to experienced Librarians Regionwise and All India Level.

Sister Esperanza has also been a recipient of an International Award on Februray 9, 1994, for all her services as Librarian at Patna Women's College, making the library of Appreciative Excellence and a Model College Library as stated by the U.G.C. Visiting Team.

At present Sister Esperanza is working as Librarian at Patna Women's College. Apart from her regular work, she is also engaged in research work on libraries in Christian Institutions, the Volume on which will be published in due time.

Concepts in Communication
Informatics & Librarianship — 65

General Editor: **S.P. Agrawal**

LIBRARY AND INFORMATION SCIENCE

Emerging Trends

Sister M. Esperanza, A.C.
Librarian
Patna Women's College
Patna

CONCEPT PUBLISHING COMPANY, NEW DELHI 110059

ISBN 81-7022-542-6

First Published 1995

Published and Printed by
Ashok Kumar Mittal
Concept Publishing Company
A/15-16, Commercial Block, Mohan Garden
NEW DELHI 110059 (India)

*I DEDICATE THIS WORK TO MY
PRINCIPAL, SISTER M. LICERIA, A.C.,
AS MY TRIBUTE OF GRATITUDE FOR
ALL THE HELP AND ENCOURAGEMENT
I HAVE RECEIVED IN MY CAREER AS
LIBRARIAN OF PATNA WOMEN'S COLLEGE*

GENERAL EDITOR'S INTRODUCTION

Not very long ago the libraries were considered as mere storehouses and unnecessary appendages to the academic institutions which were generally manned semi-educated persons or dignified clerks. Neither the efforts were made to improve their services to their users, nor the concerned authorities showed any concern for providing trained and competent staff to the libraries to run them on modern lines. Gradually, with the improvement of the schools and colleges the libraries attached to them received some attention. Now the things have changed considerably. In the past two decades there have been appreciable developments in library services, practices and techniques in all types of libraries in India. Particularly some of the university libraries and the special libraries made a phenomenal progress. They have improved both their resources and their services. There have also been vast improvements in the status of the librarians and their emoluments. Through the efforts of University Grants Commission the librarians of the colleges and the university libraries are now at par with the insofar pay scale and the status in concerned university teachers. A large number of schools of education have come up for providing library education and training to those who have chosen to work in the libraries and the information centres. They are also engaged in research work and are producing professional literature on different aspects of library and information science. Besides these, the establishment of a large number of specialised libraries on science and technology and on economic activities have also made their presence felt in the library and information world. These libraries have started introducing new information technologies in a limited scale.

Despite all these improvements that we find in our libraries and information centres they are still far behind the libraries and information centres of the industrialised nations. We have miles to go to reach them in their standard. The governmental involvement has increased no doubt, but not to the extent it is desirable. There are many reasons for the slow pace of library development. But the main reason is the inadequate provision of funds. India has the largest number of universities in the world. But the number of universities which are reasonably good in providing reading materials and library services to their users is not very large. The plight of school and college libraries is no better. Even in metropolitan cities school libraries which are manned by qualified librarians have been functioning in an unsatisfactory manner. Due to resource crunch our public libraries too are in trouble. Our library schools have failed to produce personnel who could meet the challenging needs of the organisations for which they are working. Since there is no arrangement in these schools for imparting training to their students in the use of the new communication technologies which have revolutionised the library services, their products are ignorant about the application of computer in library operations. Whatever the researches the library community has made so far are not of much significance and have generally no linkages with the professional practices. Moreover, the bulk of the professional literature produced through books and journals, seminars, conferences and symphisa does not merit much attention and lacks depth and imagination.

The present publication, which is the outcome of the authoress long experience of working in a resuted college library, provides a refreshing reading to the library community on the important aspects of the library and imformation science.The authoress has discussed the problems of the academic and public libraries in depth and with imagination. Since the impact of computers has permeated all sectors of librarianship and imformation retireval, the volume explains admirably in non-specialist manner how the computer can be used in various operations of the libraries and information centres.

The publication emphasises the need for the librarians and the information scientists not only to know the method of information retrieval but also to understand the behaviour and the information gathering pattern of the information seekers. Moreover, it is also their responsibility to make the users library-oriented, and to educate them about the different operation of the library and ways they can find out the needed information for themselves, It also pleads for resource sharing which is very essential due to limited and inadequate resources in most of our libraries and information centres. Even in the West the libraries which have enormous resources have been adopting the policy of resource sharing as no library even with its vast collection can claim self-sufficiency.

S.P. AGRAWAL

PREFACE

The volume presents a compilation of the various papers presented at seminars and conferences of Indian Library Associations (ILA), Delhi; All India Association of Christian Higher Education (AIACHE), Delhi; Indian Association of Special Libraries and Information Centres (IASLIC), Calcutta; and other Associations in India, from 1984-93. It also includes a summary of talks delivered by the authoress at various Refresher Courses organized at Government level for the Eastern and All India experienced Librarians of the school from 1991-93. The volume also summarises the talks delivered at the Workshop organized by the authoress for the Librarians of the Bihar region, at Patna Women's College Library in 1993.

Library Science being a developing field, its works are being geared more and more towards automation and technology in library development. Bihar has neither a State Library nor any law to govern the library movement in the State. The modern libraries are becoming a great source of concern to the Educational Institutions as well as to the Education Department. For, without the proper Library System, there is a deterioration of the Educational Standards.

In the past, Libraries played a very effective role in exchanging views on social issues and in giving direction to the social and political movement. However, things have changed today. The modern public and academic libraries are starved for want of proper funds. This has caused a deterioration of the services in libraries. It is time that a proper infrastructure is drawn up for the Public, College, University and School Libraries.

This work stresses on the need to make the library services more effective by updating information on the latest advances in Information Technology and Computerization.

The Public Libraries which are the peoples' libraries, are in a deplorable condition not only for lack of funds for its collections but also for their maintenance and payment of salaries to the existing staff of the library. The academic libraries have their difficulties in managing the libraries both at the College and at the University level. These libraries are not yet recongnized as necessary laboratories and that as forming a part of the Educational System. The lack of funds and personnel hinders these libraries from being serviceable to the student community. The school libraries which gain their importance of being Agents of Education during the formative years of our youth are the most neglected in the country and in the State of Bihar in particular.

My thanks to all those who have inspired and encouraged me to work on this edition. I am greatful to Sister Marie Jessie, A.C., Department of English, Patna Womn's College, who has given much of her time to go through my manuscript and has been a great source of inspiration and encouragement in helping me go ahead with the work of the manuscript.

I am also greatful to Sarojini Kumaran, my assistant in the library, who has shown great interest in this work all along.

I thank M/s Concept Publishing Company, for agreeing to undertake to publish this volume.

SISTER M. ESPERANZA, A.C.

LIST OF TABLES

LIST OF FIGURES

ABBREVIATIONS

AGRICS	:	Agricultural Information System/International Information System for Agricultural Sciences and Technology
A.E.P.	:	Adult Education Programme
A.P.	:	Andhra Pradesh
A.V.	:	Audio-Visual
C.P.U.	:	Central Processing Unit
C.A.S.	:	Current Awareness Service
D.P.I.	:	Director of Public Instruction
D.R.T.C.	:	Documentation Research and Training Centre
ENVIS	:	Environmental Information System
FCO	:	Nehru/Radhakrishnan Centenary British Scholarship/ Fellowship
HCL	:	Hindustan Computer Limited
INTREX	:	Information Transfer Exchange
ICAR	:	Indian Council of Agricultural Research
INSDOC	:	Indian National Scientific Documentation Centre
INFLIBNET	:	Information Library Network
ILA	:	Indian Library Association
IASLIC	:	Indian Association of Special Libraries and Information Centres
ICSSR	:	Indian Council of Social Science Research
IGNOU	:	Indira Gandhi National Open University
IGLA	:	International Federation of Library Associations and Institutions
LAN	:	Local Area Networks
LCC	:	Laknotic Computer Centre
MARC	:	Machine Readable Catalogue
MIT	:	Massachusetts Institute of Technology
NIC	:	National Informatics Centre
NISSAT	:	National Information System for Science and Technology
NIIT	;	National Institute of Information and Technology
OCLC	:	Ohio College Library Centre
P.R.	:	Public Relations

S.D.I.	:	Selective Dissemination of Information
UNESCO	:	United Nations Educational, Scientific and Cultural Organization
U.S.A.	:	United States of America
U.K.	:	United Kingdom
U.G.C.	:	University Grants Commission
UCL	:	Uptron Computer Limited
USSR	:	Union of Soviet Socialist Republics (now Russia)
V.C.R.	:	Video Cassette Recorder
WAN	:	Wider Area Networks

INTRODUCTION

Modern libraries are power houses of Information and Technology which has brought in many revolutionary changes. The automation in early fifties brought about possibilities for the growth of libraries through mechanization. The need for better manpower becomes all the more relevant today due to various technologies engulfing the information field.

When Education System is suffering critically these days and creating tense situations for readers and users of the library, it is a great challenge for modern libraries to keep working for efficiency and progress.

The Library System in Academic libraries has a big role to play. Considering the importance of dissemination of information in our lives and in our everyday work, the function of academic libraries becomes all the more important. The mass communication medias and audio-visual materials dominate the Educational Programmes making our academic libraries fulfil the need for information dissemination. A modern society which is a knowledge-based society depends on the production and efficient use of information through the libraries. Hence, our academic libraries at college and at University levels, have to be Research Oriented libraries. The library education provides a springboard for a life-long education.

In the context of the importance of libraries, the public library in a S' .te has also a very important role to disseminate knowledge in all the fields of learning because it is basically linked up with the social welfare of its people. A Public Library is an inseparable link with the social development. UNESCO states that 'a public library is a living force of peoples' education'.

The significance of the public library to its users will generally be demonstrated by the facilities which it offers to them. It will also be judged by the extent to which it fulfils what the readers demand of it, and by the extent to which it meets the general and any special requirements both of adults and of children.

The very name of the Public Library, poses a question before us - 'Do Public Libraries' play a role in promoting literacy among the various unlearned groups of the Indian population? Public Libraries are meant to meet the needs of the general public in various aspects of life. It is the intellectually equipped society alone that can solve its own problems by using a public library to their benefit.

The development of public libraries in our country began under the First Five Year Plan. But till now there has been very little progress or rather no progress at all in its proper functioning system. The importance of Education today is to meet the challenge of illiteracy and the need to emphasize the Adult Education Programme through the public library system. 'Learning for Earning' has become the slogan of the modern Educational System. This slogan has influenced the library functions and the library services. As a result, our libraries still remain ill-equipped, there is a lack of purchasing power and no proper reading materials are made available for readers as well as for researchers. Both the Educational System as well as the Library System in our country needs to be basically reformed to meet the modern needs of readers of all types.

In the chapters that follow, reference is made to the public Library System in particular in the State of Bihar, although, the situation of libraries in Bihar is no worse than the library situation in other parts of the country. The problems of lack of adequate funds and staff and the unconcerned attitude of those in authourity remains the same everywhere. These problems are also relevant to larger libraries in the country as well as to those outside India.

The U.G.C. has created a New Planning Commission with a Review Working Group Committee for the Eighth Plan of the Government, to look into the problems of libraries. It is not easy to find a solution to the many problems which the libraries are facing today everywhere.

Considering the importance of Public and Academic Libraries, the School Libraries are no less important. They remain neglected even to this day when efforts are being made to develop the Educational System in the country. A school library is the most strategic point in any educational institution and it compensates for poor and inefficient teaching in classrooms.

A school library is considered to be a Dynamo of stimulation currents. It is an open house for readers to browse through books for information and inspiration. What is the place of a library in a school today?

Finally, the importance and effectiveness of our libraries contsists in shaping the future of individuals during their formation years of life. It is in the library that one learns to inculcate the reading habit and acquire knowledge with one's own efforts.

Dr. S.R. Ranganathan, Father of Library Science in India, has endeavoured to make India a Library Conscious country through his painstaking efforts and his spirit of dedication to library profession. May his spirit lead us on to make our libraries, centres of information and knowledge.

1

Automation in Libraries

When we read the history of automation in the West, it is interesting to know that Library Automation began with the use of automatic and semi-automatic data processing machines. It was the Librarian Herman Hollerith who attributed his idea for a machine for tabulation work to the suggestion of Dr. John Shaw Billings. Hence the equipment for this work was invented in 1890 known as punch cards to tabulate the census figures of that particular year. The punch cards system found an entrance in libraries, through mechanized system.

Up to 1960, before the computers came into existence, library automation lagged behind when compared with the business industry and science. The lag was mainly due to lack of enthusiasm of the librarians. The capacity for data collection was small and there was no provision for data storing nor for data retrieval except on punch cards. The computers began the second era of library automation system, although the Punch Card Equipment still remained. The main reason for developing the library automation system in 1960 was due to the availability of computers and improvements in data processing.

In India, computers were used for the first time in 1960. Computer-based processing started between 1963-64, but due to non-availability of proper machines, it was not progressive. The use of computers came into force, when the literature search in Science and Technology was becoming unmanageable in libraries. SPEED and EFFICIENCY are the two key factors of information retrieval services. This can be done either by computers or by on-line information retrieval services, although the latter is more effective and speedy.

A computer consisted of INPUT, OUTPUT and PROCESSING Units (Fig. 1.1). The computer can be applied to any calculating device. It is used both for storing and for processing information.

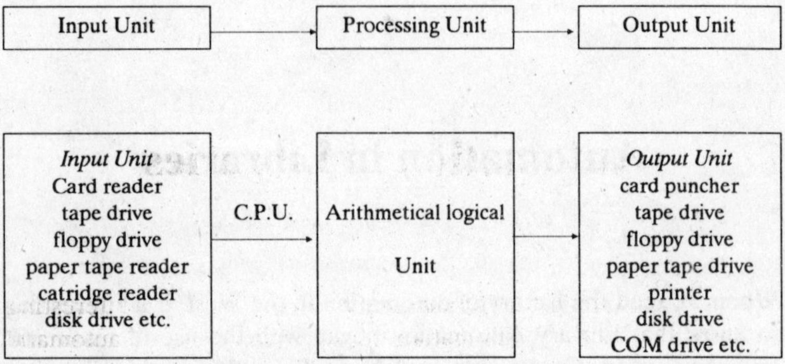

Fig. 1.1. A Computer System

Computers, whether main frame, mini frame or micro frame, are being used to speed up work in libraries. Computer networks are

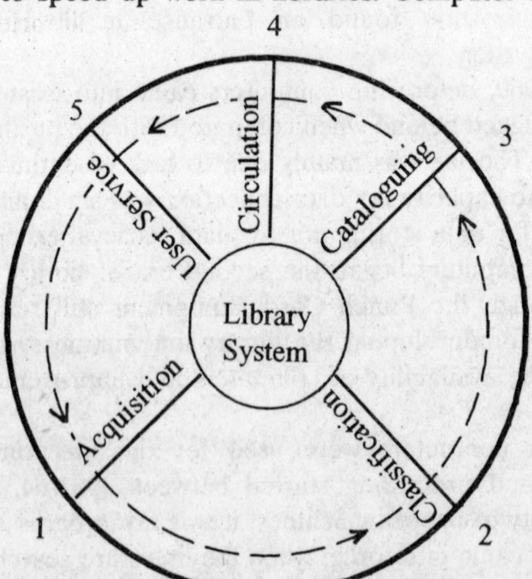

Fig. 1.2. Computer-related activities

used for effective resource sharing and for disseminating the non-available material in particular libraries. In libraries, computer activities are inter-related (Fig.1.2). No library activity stands by itself. Each activity is dependent on another for its completion. There is hardly any library operation where computers cannot play a useful role.

In the acquisition section, a simple computer programme can be written which will accept the title and other necessary Bibliographic details of a publication to be ordered and the address to whom the order is to be placed, so that the order will be printed by the computer ready to be mailed. Collection of documents is held together by cataloguing. The traditional tools used to organize collections are cataloguing and classification. Although several changes and developments have taken place in cataloguing, its definition and the function remains the same. Computer can be used for one entry record. MARC, the modern form of cataloguing produces punch paper on type recorder and catalogues are produced.

Circulation control consists mainly in record-keeping of books and other literature issued to users and what is returned by them. To manage these records in large libraries is time-consuming and an exhaustive procedure. To request for a book author-wise or title-wise, or to seek a book subject-wise is quickened by a computer system. A message to be conveyed for more than one reader is put in a computer. Computers also help in the location of information as soon as it is called for.

A computer is a useful device giving useful information regarding circulation of the reading materials:

- it shows which library document is out and who has it.
- it indicates date of issue and the possible date for its return.
- it helps to search out for missing documents.
- it allows reservation of library materials.
- it maintains records of over-due books and of reminders given.
- it helps to recall charged-out materials.

Further, the micro-computers with different programmes are also used in Circulation work. These easily show the location, condition, charged or discharged position of any document of the library. The computer efficiency has increased tremendously and are now in their fifth generation.

The users on their part are very much facilitated by the automation system in libraries. It is a time-saving device in literature search. By it the users can have a better knowledge of the library holdings. It also helps the users to make a quick choice of the needed material.

Bringing together the computer and the library is a natural alliance. A library being a place of storage of systematic knowledge and information, it facilitates the retrieval system and this is done through the computer service. INTREX and MARC is another automation system, planned in 1965 but operated in 1970. Earlier in 1945, the possibility of "MEMEX" was already visualized. This device helped to mechanize the individual stored books, records and communications with greater speed and flexibility. But than, later, with the development of the 'MIT' services the automation advanced much in the libraries of U.S.A.

In 1965, MARC created a great influence and was initiated by the library of Congress in the 20th century. Millions of machines, records and letters were used to make this service effective. These machines today have made a tremendous progress in the West in developing the National and International Information services. The success of MARC is felt in the advancement of modern technology and its services are being widely exploited in many parts of the world. MARC and INTREX laid the foundation for another era of Library Automation, namely, the introduction of on-line inter-active computer system. Through this system, the data and the programmes are delivered to the computer in MARC form and the desired output is produced. The on-line computer system and MARC have brought about Bibliographic sources on the National scale and a reference system has become essential in modern libraries, thus giving rise to a time-saving system.

After MARC, we have the off-line system which is its extension. The pilot project covered only the English language at the start, but today it has become a National Programme. The Library of Congress uses MARC and OFF-LINE Systems to experiment in cataloguing and in classification. Some of the advanced libraries follow another technique of COM for catalogue cards. But these services being geared by IBM output, it creates many problems.

The On-line cataloguing system in the development of

The network function of the library (Fig 1.3) fall under four categories, namely:

1. network level
2. processing level
3. macro-functional level
4. micro-functional level

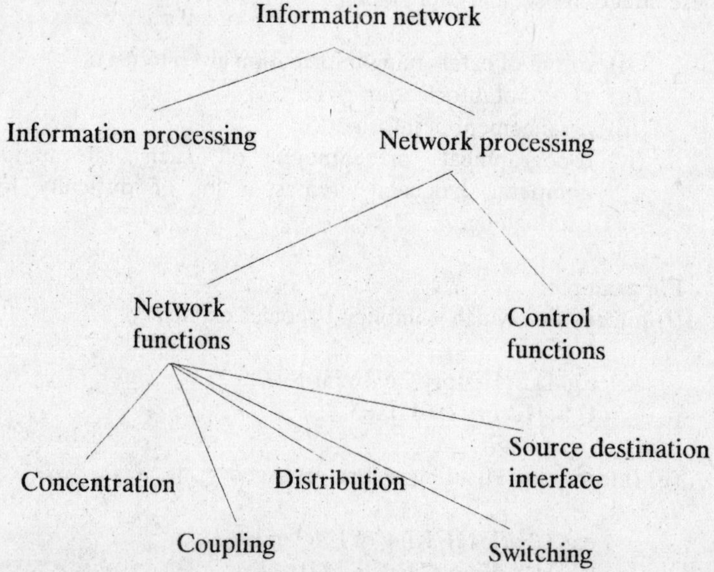

FIG. 1.3. Network Functions of the Library

OFF-LINE System and is used in acquisition system. It is a very progressive system. MARC records are converted for use in these systems and original cataloguing is done by using the terminals. On-line operations are carried on in Ohio College Library Centre (OCLC) since 1971.

Effects of Automation

Library automation refers to automated systems in libraries which include processing systems, such as:

Acquisition
Cataloguing
Serials and
Circulation

(a) Automation to some extent has affected most of the library processes and has also influenced the development of library policy. These effects are seen in cataloguing:

(i) extent of cataloguing information given to users
(ii) choice of information given
(iii) arrangement of information
(iv) topographical presentation of such information computer language creates a lot of difficulty for cataloguing.

For example;
(i) Information which is implicit becomes explicit

e.g. U.S. History Civil War :
U.S. History 1861-1865.

(ii) Information Headings get re-arranged

e.g. Charles II, King of England:
Charles, King of England II

(iii) Punctuation is a problem
(iv) Information in the headings is ignored or removed

e.g Los Angeles : Los

(b) Automation Systems are also followed in serials - in accessioning, receiving, binding and in records maintained in up-dated machine files. The cards get arranged in different sequences:

(1) By title
(2) By method of acquisition
(3) By source of acquisition

(4) By month of volume-change
(5) By month of index arrival
(6) By month of binding pick-up
(7) By year of binding
(8) By type of index
(9) By self location
(10) By type of Binding
(11) By subject
(12) By special categories-changed titles, dead titles, etc.

Off-Line computer listing can also be done for numbering of serials.

(c) Automated Systems in Circulation systems have been most successful than in any other type of library system. The reason for this is because :

- operations are repeatitive
- procedures are systematic
- circulation can easily be separated from other library activities.
- Bibliographic information used need not be extensive
- Programming problems are not complex

The Circulation systems manipulate three kinds of information

(i) information about borrower (address, name, etc.)
(ii) information about material borrowed (call No., author, title, etc.).
(iii) information about the loan itself (date due, time of loan).

All this information can be collected in various ways; for example, it can be written by the borrower or by the clerk and then put into the system. After the collection of the required information, the following fuctions identifies the location of network functions relating to information network architecture.

(1) Provision of information on the location of circulating items - (bindery, reserve, storage, re-cataloguing).
(2) Identification of items on loan (off campus, users).

(3) Recording of personal reserves desired by borrowers - (to notify about book availability).
(4) Printing recall notices on long-term loans
(5) Renewal of loans
(6) Notification of over-due items to staff
(7) Notification to staff of delinquent borrowers - (unpaid fines, over-due books).
(8) Calculation of fines and printing of fine receipts.
(9) Calculation and printing of statistics of various types.
(10) Analysis of summary statistics for circulation.
(11) Provision for handling special book or reading material to borrowers.

A few systems also print data-due slips,

e.g. systems at Johns Hopkins University Library - for *charging* books, place books in a tray, spines to the front with student identification card.

More on-line systems have been installed in foreign countries for calculation control than for any other purpose.

Problems of Library Automation Systems

The automation system has both merits and demerits. But often, the demerits are not given importance. Demerits in automation system involve two groups of three factors each :

Group 1 - PEOPLE :

(i) at the computer centre
(ii) Systems personnel, suppliers of hardware and software
(iii) Librarians

Group 2 - PROBLEMS :

(i) Poor Planning
(ii) Poor designing
(iii) Poor implementation

Prospects of Library Automation Systems

Recent history of library automation systems is characterized by several strong trends brought about by changes both in technology and in the economic situation confronting libraries today. Unless radical changes in these two areas are dealt with, the trends will continue to dominate and determine the library automation development for some time to come.

The main changes are the library networks i.e. systems involving more than one library. Library networks come in many forms. The most common is the Cooperative Centre for providing catalogue cards. OCLC is a good example.

The development of standards has also facilitated the networking systems. MARC is the National Standard for machine-readable Bibliographical Data. It is a most successful standard in networks. The future success of automation system can be assured only through having standards. There will be very little change in the near future in card production. Instead, most of the libraries will adopt the network systems for cataloguing and for resource sharing. Many of the college and University libraries have not yet opened their doors to let the computer in. But when technology advances and the break-through comes, the library profession will be ready to accept the automated systems and put them to right and effective library use.

In U.K. and in U.S.A. there has been a rapid growth of automation in College and University libraries during these recent years building its framework on minicomputer. This growth has not yet developed in India due to the financial pressures. There has been a re-thinking in many of our Indian libraries to invite computer services at the college and University level. These being service libraries, they offer quality services. Some college libraries can even be listed as special libraries because they aim at having a special library standard of service to users. In such libraries, information retrieval, specific enquiry answering, user education, CAS and SDI services are a common feature. These libraries also have a special document collection for the specific mode of the parent institutions.

The college libraries in the Western countries, with their initial attempts at experiencing the handling of non-book media, are led into electronic information services. The libraries handling tapes, slides, records, videos and the rest, step into on-line information retrieval services to the users. The on-line services can be more effective if collections of Abstracting services and primary journals are restricted.

The Fifth Law of Library Science gives the vital character of a library – "Library is a Growing Organism". The truth of this Law is experienced with all its modern forms of automated services. The law urges the librarians to keep themselves alert to the changing needs of the modern society if the libraries have to act as Agents of social change. To meet the demands of this law in the present context, there is need to be far-sighted in the planning of library buildings and the library services. These have to be geared towards the utilization of the State of Arts Computers.

Automation in libraries refers to the processing of the routine library functions and to handle large quantities of information more efficiently with the use of computers and other automated gadgets, like micro reprographic services, micro films, micro fiche, the VCR, Xeroxing services and so on.

Modern libraries are power houses of information and technology which has brought in many revolutionary changes. The introduction of computers in early fifties brought about the possibilities for the growth of the libraries through mechanization. The public library in Trivandrum (Tamil Nadu) is a clear example of this. Much before computers were spoken of, the courageous librarian of this library introduced electronic equipment to its library work to meet the increased needs of its users. Today a large number of books are micro-filmed for the preservation of the document. The newspapers too are micro-filmed from time to time to save space on the shelves. A micro-film Projector of 16mm costing Rs. four lakhs is also installed and the micro-fiche is worked on the projecting screen of the same projector. The work of processing the film is done on another complicated machine costing Rs. 1.5 lakhs and with a Printer Duplicator attached. After processing, the films are placed on the micro-film Reader of 35mm for projection.

The American Library at Delhi is another example of automation. The library uses computerized catalogues and MARC Catalogue cards. It maintains computer tools and electronic typewriters for its library works. Its secret being:

"TRANSFER KEY WORDS TO KEY SOURCES".

Computer networks have developed communications like,

telecommunication system which is today advanced Coaxial Cables, Optical Fibres, Laser Beams, Micro-wave Communication and Satellite Communication. Through all these networks, there is an increase in quality quantum in transmitted data. The facilities in communication can be put on on-line computer-based information. The modern term used is "COMPUNICATION". This data-base through compunication is scattered all over the country through Telecommunication system under the computerized networks.

Modern libraries have to get acquainted through these new changes or else, they will not survive. The time is not far when India too like other countries in the West will have to come in contact with:

(a) Information Generation or Generators
(b) Information Users
(c) Information Vendors.

Are our libraries in India ready for this change?

It is time that the college and the University libraries in the country started automation in library works and speed up the research work. It is indeed a dream of the future ! But this vision can be made a REALITY of the present only if the possibility of extensive funds and the increase of library personnel is made available. It is only then that the libraries at all levels in the country, will be able to render efficient services and keep pace with the advances of modern technology in the changing modern society.

UNESCO is actively engaged in a World Information System called "the United System of Information". In order to make the future libraries in India, Information Centres, the departments of Science and Technology have given the Government of India, the responsibility to frame the National Information System for Science and Technology. The ESRIN Centre in Italy which provided Bibliographical references via Satellites, has already demonstrated a Project at Bombay. This experiment was the activity of UNESCO, forming an integral part of a wider programme of UNISIST through a link development to developed countries in the world of Science and Technology.

It was almost two decades ago that studies in computer and telecommunication were started in India. No doubt a lot of progress has been made. India was one of the first few nations which realized the potentialities of computers for Bibliographical information work and routine library operations. But all these efforts today have borne very little fruit. Instead of more and more institutions going in for automation, there is a growing indifference among librarians. The result is, that modern libraries are not able to catch up with the speed of development of automation and information works.

2

Information Technology in Libraries

Every human need depends on information for its fulfilment. In all ages human beings have been dependant on information and communication either in oral or in written form. It is estimated that 70 per cent of time is spent in communication by every human being and today we find that a great number of people are employed in information activities.

The history of man-made information technology was of slow evolution and dates back to about 5,000 years. Later this developed in alphabetical writing, printing and computer typesetting technology. In recent years we have the development of not only telephones and radio but television, satellite transmission, the computer and the micro-processor which represent qualitative changes in information technology. The very fact that we have to accept the term information technology includes a whole range of new developments.

Information technology is nothing but the science of information handing. Computers are used to support the communication of knowledge in technical, economic and social fields. UNESCO defines information technology as :

> "Scientific, technological and engineering disciplines and the management techniques used in information handling and processing: their application, computers and their interaction with men and machines and associated social, economic and cultural matters."

This definition emphasises the significant role of computers. But the communication systems are as essential to information technology as computers. As a result we have three branches of technology -

Computer,
Micro-electronics, and
Communications.

Information Technology is a recent and comprehensive term, which describes the whole range of processes, which have been at work without human intervention throughout the process of organic evolution. For example, in the reproduction systems of all species of creation, with the genetic transmission of information from generation to generation and the evolution of the brains and the central nervous system.

The introduction of new technologies is causing rapid change in printing industry. The dominating factors in this industry are the computers, microprocessors, lasers and screen-based technology including television and telecommunications. With the advent of computers, compact disks and on-line facilities, the Information Industry has developed tremendously. Application of computers in information storage and information retrieval is catching fast. Computers and telecommunication are the main components of Information Technology and their influence in information storage and dissemination is immense. These two components also help to meet the problems of information explosion.

The advancement in electronic printing technology today has enabled the printing of information on magnetic and optical discs. Laser beams are being used for printing the entire 32 volumes of *Encyclopaedia Britannica* on pin head.

The word LIBRARY becomes meaningless in this era of information technology. Rather a more fitting term to be used for our modern libraries would be "Information Centres". Often knowledge is spoken of as 'Power' and 'A Mighty Sword' and it is knowledge with all its power that is responsible today for the present social, cultural, religious, spiritual, scientific, technological and materialistic world that we are living in. It is only the intellect in a human being that can acquire this knowledge without resources of information. Information is storage of knowledge and also its foundation.

Mikhailov, the Russian Scientist, is the first man to coin the term information and to define it. Information is nothing else but knowledge. This knowledge can be obtained from information given in one para or one page, and this knowledge helps us to solve our problems, find out solutions to our doubts and problems and also to take decisions. Information which is generated by research is growth in information and this is known as information explosion or information revolution.

Through Information Technology easy methods are developed for information retrieval, storage, dissemination and communication. The two great concepts in the Scientific world today are Information Technology and Information Industry. Although Information Technology is a recent term, it is rapidly getting popular among the various disciplines by a micro-electronics based combination of computing-tele-communications, even in our libraries. 'Information Technology' is understood by many as the 'New Technology'.

Information technology in its strictest sense is a new science to collect, to store, to process and to transmit information. Computers can promote information needs of the society in its economic conditions better and more effectively. This technology is also concerned to promote information through books, print, reprography and other networks. In this aspect the application of technology gains its importance in our libraries in India.

Libraries as Information Centres have to have access to the available information in the world. This is possible only through the development of telecommunication technology along with computer technology, which helps in effective resource sharing, networking and on-line information retrieval from data bases.

The major problem for library computerisation in developing countries like India is the high cost of computer machine and the software packages. The cost of software rises 10 per cent every year while the cost of hardware tends to decrease faster. Another problem is that software packages are not all portable.

The conglomeration of computers, databases and telecommunication has created information networks, which facilitate sharing of library resources and services as well. In addition, these information networks are also connected with the international information systems. Networks can refer to the Local Area Networks (LAN) or Wider Area Networks (WAN). The

'Ontime Computer Library Centre' (OCLC), the 'International Nuclear Information Service' (INIS), the 'International System for Agricultural Science and Technology' (AGRIS) is another network area in which India is participating and it provides the national INPUT to the system. In turn, it gets the AGRIS output magnetic tapes. The Indian Agricultural Statistics Research Institute, which is a part of ICAR, has started a SDI service with computer programmes developed locally using AGRIS Tapes. At present, the SDI service is open to scientists working in ICAR institutes and agricultural universities.

The National Informatics Centre (NIC) has taken up the major project of developing an integrated information system for the Government of India. The efforts to design the system with all the needed software have yielded results and it has been stated that the entire project is in a take-off stage. The NIC effort is one of the major steps in developing computer-based information systems in our country.

INSDOC was perhaps the first in experimenting with computers to harness them for developing information products and services.

Another successful network is the 'British Library Automated Information Service' (BLAISE). The British Library plans to make books available to its readers through terminals that will access on the On-time Public Access Catalogue (OPAC). Although funds are limited, 150 OPAC terminals would be available in the next few years.

Since the past five years, Library and Information activities in our country has entered a new area of development. A great number of Library Resource Sharing Networks like at Calcutta (CALIBNET), at Delhi (DELNET), at Ahmedabad (ADONET), and research laboratories like CSIR are under various stages of development.

Where academic libraries are concerned, we have a long way to go before we make our libraries automated. However, U.G.C. has taken a bold step forward in establishing a computer-based library resource sharing network called (INFLIBNET) - information and library network programme which will be implemented during the Eighth Fifth Plan Period (1990-1995). Under this scheme a national centre will be set up at Delhi with four Regional Centres.

In the late sixties and early seventies several Research Laboratories were established in the country. This led to rise in demand for trained librarians and they were recruited and given pay-scales and status equivalent to or near equivalent to scientists. The National Libraries-Sectoral (Specialised) Information Centres: realizing that Information is power and a national resource, a trend has now emerged to create network of libraries by information centres in the country in various especialized fields like drugs, and pharmaceuticals, food science and technology, small-scale industries, environment and toxic chemical, machine tools, textiles, aeronautics, social science and many more (Figs. 2.1 and 2.2).

Level 0	Level 1	Level 2	Level 3	Level 4
	Fishery Food crops Cash crops Livestock *meat* *poultry* *dairy*	Food Beverages: Tobacco *Textiles* Clothing Footwear	Chemicals Petroleum & Coal products Basic chemicals Fertilizer Paints, inks, Explosives, Pesticides,	Vehicle Manufacutre Road Rail Sea Waterways Air
	Forestry	Wood, Wood products Paper, Paper products	Soaps, Phar- maceuticals, cosmetics, Liquid fluids, lubricants	
Energy Wood Bio-gas Wind	*Mining* Quarrying	Iron & Steel Non Ferrous Metal	Wood & Metal Craft Work	Electrical Goods Components Equipments
Oil Electricity Thermal Hydel Nuclear		Non Mettalic Mineral Products Glass, Glass Products	Printing & Publishing Fabricated Metal products	Electronic goods
Fusion Solar		Bricks, ceramics cement, concrete plaster, storeware	Metal containers Tools, Nuts & Bolts Sprint & wire Products	Components Equipments
			Rubber and plastic products	Electronic Systems Communication Computers
			Production Technology Goods	
			CAM Robotics	Manual N.C.

Fig 2.1. Primary and Secondary Production Sector Industries

Figure 2.1 is a disturbing picture of production base in India.

Figure 2.1 is a disturbing picture of production base in India. This can be better appreciated if we look at the various service inputs that sustain primary and secondary production sectors in a industrialized economy (Fig 2.2).

For managing and operating these information centres and network, trained manpower in library and information science are needed.

With the increasing need for specialised information, a greater awakening has been felt to share this resource by joining hands with libraries and information centres to form a network and to use computers and communication technology for speedy diversification of information and reaching the same to remotest possible places (Fig. 2.3). Several sectoral information centres under the National Information System in Science and Technology (NISSAT), National

Construction Builidngs Watersupply Seweage Roads Rail tracks Canals & Waterways 1, 3, 5	Management Planning & Research Administration Marketing – Advertisement – Other Promotion Sales Wholesale Retail 1, 2, 4	Finance Banks Insurance Ral Estate Stock Exchange 2, 3, 4
Transportion & Storage Rail, Road, Sea, Air Inland Waterways Vehicle – operation – Maintenance Warehousing 1, 2, 3, 4	Primary Production Secondary	Communications Posts, Telegraphs, Telex, Telephones Digital Data Equipment – Operation – Maintenance 3, 6, 7
Recreation & Tourism Cinema, TV, Radio Audio, Sports, Racing Clubs, Hotels, Restaurants, Travel Agencies 2, 3, 4	Social overheads Government National, State, Local – City – Ward – Village Law & Order Police Prevention Detection Justice Defence 1, 3, 4	Community services Education & Basic Research Health, Human, Veterinary – Paramedical – Testing & Diogniosis – Hospital care Libraries, Museums., Galliries Weather services Personal artisan services 3, 4, 5, 7

Fig. 2.2. The Service Sector "Industries"

	USA	UK	Japan	India
Relative land area	39	1	1.5	14
Relative population	4	1	2	11 (1976)
Books: No. of different titles published-1973	83724	35179	35857	14064
Newspapers (1972)				
No. of Dailies	1761	109	172	793
Circulation/1000 persons	297	528	519	16
Other periodicals	9755	4669	6241	7080
Circulation/1000 persons	n.a.	n.a.	n.a.	29
Films : Feature films	280 (1970)	89 (1972)	423 (1970)	414 (1970)
Annual attendance per person	5	2.4	1.7	6.2
Radio : Transmitters	6719 (1971)	397 (1972)	911 (1974)	132 (1973)
Receivers/1000 persons	1752 (1973)	697 (1972)	658 (1972)	24 (1973)
Television: (1973) Receivers/1000 persons	523	30	229	0.3
Telephone : (1975-1976) Sets/1000 persons	718	394	427	3
Mail : (1971) No. per person per annum (all kinds of mail)	416	191	115	12 (1978)

Fig. 2.3 : Levels of Information Consciousness

Social Science Documentation Centre; (INFLIBNET), Information Library Network; (ENVIS), Environmental Information System, and many more have been created to share information and effect speedier communication with the help of computers, electronic mail, fax and telex. The National Information Centre under the Department of Electronics has created the largest network known as 'National Information Centre Network' with an information centre in each district in the country.

Further, the level of information consciousness in India compared with other developed countries – USA, U.K. and Japan, as is seen in Fig. 2.4, we have not been growing an industrial and a professional culture. How could we change this low information consciousness? How could we transform our culture into a truly industrial and professional one? The only answer would be that we make imaginative use of information technology which we lack and which we need to build up our level of information consciousness.

In India we look to the West to derive inspiration and ideas for industrializing and modernizing ourselves and yet we can learn much of immediate relevance by looking to the East and studying Japan more closely. Japan is a living example to the fact that a country need not be self-sufficient in resources in order to become a world leader in trade and industry. Japan has demonstrated to us that through implementation of technology we can have a leading industry.

The need for better manpower becomes all the more relevant today due to various technologies engulfing the information field. Every library professional has to be sensitive to the environment of information and be receptive to the developments in the Educational field and scientific environment. The only way to give our libraries a proper professional skill is by a continuous up-dating of knowledge. The progress of our libraries depends very much on the efficiency of librarians who are the managers of the libraries responsible for the whole functioning order of the library.

Institutions of Higher Learning in India are the fountain springs of Education. These institutions have a reason to be proud of their libraries which have a key role to play in Higher Educational Programmes in our country. These libraries are the sources of vital information for academic and research students. During the past three decades the quality of library manpower has improved to a great extent with a good theoretical knowledge of Library and Information Science.

The Education System of today suffering critically, and creating tense situations for the readers and users of libraries, is a great challenge for modern Librarians. A librarian is the ANCHOR-MAN, a position demanding an unwavering austerity and veracity. There are always gaps between Research and Development and Every-day practice. The only solution to meet this need is Continuing Education (See Fig. 2.4) which involves all the learning activities for library staff after their initial Library Education.

The best library education can become obsolete in a few years, unless there be a determined effort to continue the on-going

Education (Bell, 1979). Continuing Education not only prevents obsolescence, but it provides a psychological back-up to cope with the changes coming from the society and from technology. These changes eventually get embodied into the recorded literature with which the librarian is expected to deal with.

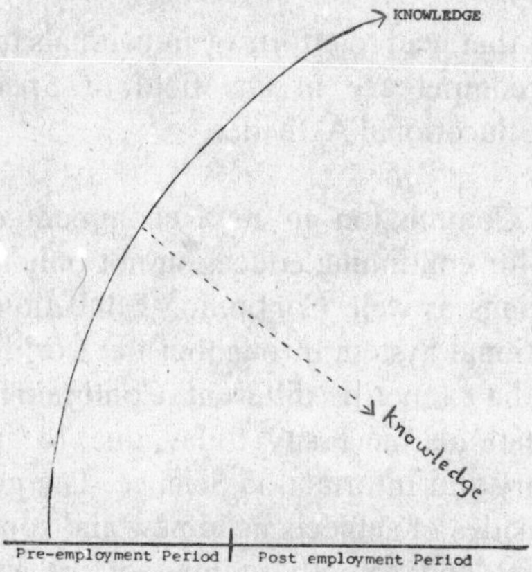

Fig. 2.4: Curve of Knowledge

Continuing Education is essential for all library personnel working in all types of libraries - Public, Academic or Special Libraries. The Continuing Education could have a variety of programmes such as:

– Academic up-dating
– Library techniques
– Library management
– Users Studies
– Information technology
– Research and Development
– Public relations

The success of these programmes depends largely on the cooperation from the Government authorities as there is need for funds to organize the continuing education activities.

The basic need for continuing education is, that it focuses attention of some well-known topics like;

– Education is not a once-for-all process
– No one is too old to learn
– No one is too knowledgeable to know

The A.L.A. guidelines define Continuing Eduction as,

> "all activities that lead to efforts by individuals to upgrade one's knowledge, competence in any field of Specialization, are Continuing Educational Activities."

The Kothari Commission in its Recommendations also has stressed the need for continuing education not only for teachers but also for all Librarians as well. Continuing Education has become a part of the Educational System throughout the world since 1960 and the situation in India cannot be different. Continuing Education has also become a national necessity today due to interdisciplinary approach of Library and Information Science. The growing libraries with all its complexities of subjects need new and sophisticated skills for its management and smooth running of the various types of libraries and their works.

S.I. Malan in one of the Educational Issues states: that Librarians are primarily responsible for one's own Continued Education which one achieves not merely by attending organized library activities and by contributing to the proceedings in various ways and so on. But by being faithful readers of the professional literature and keeping themselves in constant touch with the new developments as for the purpose of study with an aim to acquire higher qualifications.

A National Institute for Continuing Education in Library and Information Science may be visualized and should be responsible for taking note of the latest developments in Library and Information Science and also of future possibilities. The Institute could also launch programmes focusing attention on formal short-term training on the changing patterns and current problems facing the modern libraries. The Institute could also sponsor projects on Continuing Education, interdisciplinary research and provide support for publications.

The advent of Information Technology and its rapid advance has made it vital to hold intensive programmes for training the professionals in the use of new automated equipments and computer systems. A working librarian has to face changes and challenges that may come up during his working period. Surveys reveal that working professionals feel within five years of entry into the profession that they have not had enough emphasis during their training on practical aspects of the profession.

Apart from the changes, a profession often faces other types of changes. The discipline of the profession may be of a fast developing nature. New ideas, new theories and new techniques may sometimes render earlier training inadequate to meet the modern changes. The library being a social institution, its services depend and are shaped by a variety of social activities, social needs and social changes. In recent years, there have been many social changes and many of them have arisen from the increasing use of new technologies. The most significant of these new range of technologies is, perhaps, the use of computer supported by new telecommunication technologies, which has changed the library and information field, with a promise of further change. These fast new ranges of changes have given rise to a felt need of some method of continuing education to cope with the new situation.

In the late sixties, Dr. S.R. Ranganathan, theoretically established the case of Librarians as professionals. While expecting 'high intellectual ability' from them, he defined their role as "to inform, educate and inspire intellectuals and to provide intellectual entertainment to all". He thus identified the core of the professional work and warned the Librarians in the following terms:

> "the calling of librarians does not become a profession merely on the ground of using electronic gadgets, like the computers or of doing reprographic work and thus using the inventions of technologists. The Role of Library Professionals today is considered: 'LIBRARIANS as TEACHERS'."

Often informal methods of continuing education are sort for by library professionals and information scientists for the sake of convenience. Formal methods are more effective. Information Technology and its rapid advances have necessitated computer and other automated systems for library functions. Continuing Education is no longer important merely for self-development but as a national need. It is necessary for effective management of libraries and Information Centres which in turn are essential for information transfer as well as for effective decision-making.

3

Role of College and University Libraries

The Educational system today is being challenged even by the Educationalists themselves. There have been several experiments and formulation of the National Education Policy of 1968 to meet the challenges. In 1985 another awakening took place through the formation of the New Education Policy for the country. To meet the demands of this awareness, educational institutions of diverse patterns and characters increased in various dimensions. With all these efforts, what came to the forefront was the lack of Quality Education.

The New Education Policy sought to reshape the whole Education structure in order to build a dynamic nation for the 21st century. This Policy was laid down as "Approach to Education Re-Orientation" neglecting the role of libraries in Education. The absence of libraries created a sensation among the library professionals. To reform the error, the Raja Rammohun Roy Library Foundation together with other Library Associations, like, the I.L.A. and IASLIC, prepared a document to bring about a library awareness. As a result, the Government appointed a Committee to draw up a National Policy and Information System to make Education more effective.

In this context, the role of libraries has become important today but its growth is still slow. Living in an age of information, we realize that information is a vast and an inexhaustible source that affects not only all the disciplines, but the lives of all the people as well.

Information forms a vital source of socio-economic development due to the fast societal changes that are taking place in the modern world. Modern libraries today are considered to be the important sources of information. For its proper dissemination, this information has to be organized. The very service of information dissemination is a source which helps the development of the nation. Information today is growing in various dimensions and our libraries must help in its growth and progress by setting up information sections and becoming as Library Information Centres to the readers.

Considering the importance of dissemination of information in our lives and in our day to day work, there is a great need to start information dissemination in our various academic libraries by identifying needs of the users. The emphasis of information together with library collection development in modern libraries is on the access to information. Mass Communication and Audio Visual materials dominate the Educational Programmes, making our libraries fulfil the need for information dissemination. We are today with a knowledge-based society which depends on the production and efficient use of information through the libraries. Unfortunately, we are met with a crisis arising from the cost of production and the problem of processing of the documents. This crisis is growing more rapidly than the budgets for the development of libraries. Traditional techniques and old techniques cannot cope with the growth of production. Changes must take place if libraries are to keep pace with the increasing volume of information.

The development of college and university libraries is closely linked with the development of Education. During the First Five Year Plan (1947-1982), libraries were developed under the pressure of Higher Education. On the other hand, the Higher Education got its priority only after Independence. Due to the division and re-organisation into linguistic States, there came a felt need for the creation of more colleges and Universities. And so, after independence, colleges mushroomed without proper preparation and planning. A few of them still exist not only with ill-equipped libraries but also other unfulfilled needs which affect the quality of teaching in them.

The old concept of libraries, that of being store houses with the Librarian as its custodian, still prevails in some parts of the country. This concept has to give way to a completely new awareness, namely, that of the libraries being an academic centre for learning. Such a centre requires functions of qualified library staff to guide the users to a proper use of its holdings.

The potential of college and University libraries can support the curriculum and provide a spring-board for a life-long education. A library is an institution whose objective is to render service to all. Any college library mirrors in its size and scope very closely to that of the parent institution. This size and scope is also concerned on the reasonable levels of expenditure, staffing pattern and accommodation of knowledge standards. What can be achieved through a good and effective library service is not obvious. However, achievement is an important perception and an healthy tradition within the college library. To bring about effective library services, their is need of close cooperation between the librarian and the college authorities.

Influence of Libraries on Education (1800-1924)

Since 1980 there has been a considerable change both in the educational system and in that of the academic libraries. Compared with the library system that prevailed during the ancient, medieval and pre-independence period, we find a vast difference today.

Ancient India could boast of excellent libraries at Taxila, the intellectual Capital of Indian Higher Education. These libraries contained works on Hinduism, Political Science, Literature, Medicine and Philosophy. The other centres of Learning at the time were the Buddhist institutions of Nalanda, Vallabhai, Vikramasila, and Odanta Puri. These institutions maintained libraries to serve as Educational Laboratories. The early development in libraries came about in 1800 when Marquis of Wellesley, the than Governor General of British India, started the Fort William College at Calcutta.

The progress of libraries and the Educational System was greatly affected by the wars during the medieval period. From 1800 to 1947, the progress of libraries remained non-progressive. There were colleges at this time without libraries and there seemed to be no effort to establish any libraries except for a few that were started in 1850. It was only after the Magna Carta of English Education in India, that libraries were given an importance. The college libraries were than revived to some extent with the establishment of

Universities of Learning at Bombay, Calcutta and Madras. These Universities were modelled on the University of London. The revival of libraries brought about a realization of they being an integral part of the Educational System. But due to lack of funds and interest on the part of the authorities, these libraries failed to grow and to make progress.

The Hunter's Commission of 1882 and the Raleigh Commission of 1902 did discover the importance of libraries in the Educational System. Accordingly, 1917 the British Government in India drew up a Report encouraging the growth of college and University libraries. The Report laid stress on the library activities with the suggestion that they be Research Oriented. In spite of all this advancement, the library facilities still remained poor. In 1948, the Government of India appointed various Committees and Commissions to study the situation of libraries in the country with the aim of improving the educational facilities. The change came about only after 1953. In 1957 the U.G.C. team conducted surveys which brought to light more forcefully the existence of the libraries. The surveys revealed that the existing libraries were ill-equipped and inadequate.

Surveying the Radhakrishnan Commission of 1948 and the Kothari Commission of 1964-66, it was observed that no librarian was included in the list of its committee members. For, it is only a Library Expert who could have presented an exact picture of the library system that existed at the time in the country.

It is true that college and University libraries form the central organ around which the activities of Higher Education rotate. But this statement poses two question before us:

(a) Why did college and University libraries develop as they did and play an unimportant part in the Educational System in the early 19th century?

(b) What are the problems facing the college and the University libraries of today?

Going back to the Charter Act of 1813, we read that Lord Minto visualized that the importance and necessity of college libraries came to the forefront along with the importance of college education. The turning point in the history of the progress of libraries and education was brought about in 1835 with the promotion of English literature and Science. The allocation of adequate funds by the

Recommendations of the Hunter Commission, towards the Educational facilities also went a long way to strengthen the position of libraries of this period. Towards 1939, the libraries did begin to develop but this progress was at a very slow speed.

The College and University libraries make a meaningful contribution to the Quality of Education and offer a challenging career pattern to students. Modern libraries help its users to step into the world of adventure and learning. Both college and University libraries are themselves above all else, an enormous source of learning. As such, they have a vital task before them in Education. This task is to encourage the concept of learning as a potentially enjoyable life-long process. To make the library services effective, every library is in need of co-ordination and co-operation of the teaching staff. Computerization in libraries, the computerized systems and the new communication media, has changed the concept of modern libraries. In such libraries even the college librarian has an important role to play in the process of modern education.

Development of Libraries

During the pre-independence period, although libraries were considered to be important, the library services remained insignificant due to inadequate facilities for library training. The library profession did not seem to attract the best talent in the country. The recognition of library schools came about only when priority was given to Education. The U.G.C. at this time upheld the cause of libraries and encouraged library training in view of the future importance of libraries to Education in the country. The other factors that took library education forward, were the increased demands for advanced and research studies. Also an increased awareness of the need for quality library service made the library education a necessity.

The Sergent Report of 1944 from the Central Advisory Board was a Master Plan for the development of the National Educational System in the country. Unfortunately, this plan having no room for the improvement of the library system, libraries seemed to have no role in the Education of the country. Even today the Government authorities in several States do not seem to be convinced yet of the important role that college and University libraries claim in the process of Education.

Later, during the 20th century, the libraries were somewhat well organized. But the problems created in 1916 still remained. As such, the Quality Education was sacrificed for Quantity Education. In 1927, the Simon Commission appointed the Hartog Committee to study the conditions of both Education and that of the libraries in the country. It was reported by the Committee that the improper teaching methodology created hindrances for the establishment of efficient college libraries. This made the management of college libraries inadequate and without proper resources.

The New Educational System with its new concept of library management and library services does demand for trained hands to manage college and University libraries. There is also today a need for a specialized training for Librarians for the various library services, in different types of libraries, such as, Information dissemination services, Documentation services, Bibliographical services and so on. The non-existence of proper training programmes has made the Librarians incompetent to convince the authorities of the need and importance of libraries in the Education Curriculum. There had been at least two attempts to organize library training programmes. But these programmes with their limitations created a greater need for a proper training of librarians. Due to lack of proper training, the libraries came to be placed in the background. This caused a lack of proper physical facilities, staff and funds for effective library functions.

In 1919, Sir Gooroo Das Banerjee, one of the Judges of Calcutta High Court, gave the following statement as his evidence regarding the libraries in India :

> "Libraries should not be made costly
> They should not aim at having all books,
> But be content with the best of books."

This statement of Sir Gooroo is no doubt practical and it emphasizes the need to having good libraries.

Between 1940 and 1950 there had been a lot of development of libraries in the country. The progress of this development after 1950 resulted in better pay-scales for the Librarians. But this development was brought about without any planning. It has been more of a quantitative rather than a qualitative development. For the library services to be qualitative, every library has to work for more funds, more space and adequate staff. To do this, the college and University libraries in our country still lack the Leadership to take the libraries forward, they lack up-to-dateness in the building up of library collections and they lack the use of modern medias for the dissemination of knowledge.

The college and University libraries in the Educational System are easier to use and to understand and are less intimidating to the user. The Central Advisory Board of Education of 1920 with its revival in 1935 and again in 1937, dealt with the Educational problems relating to collection of literature in the college libraries in various States. In 1938, the Wood Abbot Committee studied the financial situation of the library system. It recommended larger grants for the improvement of libraries. But this Recommendation went unheeded and libraries had to suffer with their problems.

In 1945, the U.G.C. having come into existence, it helped the Government in the planning work of the Education. At this time, the majority of the College libraries were still struggling to get a better recognition. Their major problems included of having small collections, limited budgets, poor physical facilities and lack of professional staff to make the college libraries to be the central organs of the colleges. Through all these struggles the library movement in the 19th century had grown into a kind of a force by 1947 when India became an independent country. The U.G.C. Five Year Plans (see Table. 3.1) brought a closer link between the pattern of Education and the Library System.

It is unfortunate that Education today has been thought of without looking out for an Agency which can serve as a centre for the communication of ideas and for the dissemination of information. An Educational System without libraries cannot bring about a social transformation. If Education has to be of the right kind, then it has to be a library-centred education. There has to be the unification of the classroom work with that of the library work. For Education to be an on-going education, the library is the only place where one can self-educate oneself for a life-long education.

Compared to the Fourth and Fifth Five Year Plans, we find the expenditure percentage of education budget for Sixth Five Year Plan has come very low. But for Seventh and Eighth Five Year Plans the Education Budget has gone up again. The Seventh and the Eighth Five Year Plans included besides Education all types of projects. But where education is concerned there is not much improvement and there does not seem to be any hope for an increase in Education Budget in the near future.

Table 3.1. Expenditure on Education during the Five Year Plan Period

	Plans	Expenditure in crores of Rs. (1 crore is 10 million rupees)	Percentage of total Education Budget
First	Five Year Plan (1951-1956)	Rs. 140	9
Second	Five Year Plan (1956-1961)	Rs. 480	18
Third	Five Year Plan (1961-1966)	Rs. 870	15
Fourth	Five Year Plan (1969-1974)*	Rs. 195	25
Fifth	Five Year Plan (1974-1978)	Rs. 292	22.7
Sixth	Five Year Plan (1980-1984)**	Rs. 265	14
Seventh	Five Year Plan (1985-1989)***	Rs. 348	not available
Eighth	Five Year Plan (1990-1995)	Rs. 792	not available

* Forth Five Year Plan was delayed by 3 years

** Sixth Five Year Plan was cut short by 1 year

*** Seventh Five Year Plan has not seen much improvement.

The Sixth Five Year Plan laid emphasis on the quality improvement in Education through the establishment of a proper library system. The actual problem that stands in the way of Education and the library system today is that the Recommendations of the various Commissions have not been followed effectively. The U.G.C. has done much to further the progress of Education and of the library system in the country since its existence. Better scales of pay have been framed to qualified librarians bringing them on par with the teaching staff. The U.G.C. has also allotted several grants to help the college and University libraries to grow and improve their standards. But the grants allotted so generously have not helped the libraries due to non-availability of the matching share from the State Governments. To solve this problem, the U.G.C. now sanctions the Basic Grants directly to the colleges for the purchase of books and periodicals and for the improvement of libraries and its facilities and services. But the college libraries still find the grants to be insignificant in order to build up a valuable collection growth, due to the exorbitant rising prices of books and periodicals. However it is these meagre grants that have helped to bring the decaying library system to life again. Besides the above grants, the U.G.C. has also allotted grants for separate college library buildings or for their extension purpose during the Sixth Five Year Plan Period.

The survey of a few college libraries in Bihar shows that the library system needs to be strengthened so as to make them active social institutions to meet the needs of the modern society. Some libraries having good collections cannot function efficiently due to lack of staff and other library facilities for its users. In almost all the college libraries in Bihar, the collections remain under closed access and the users remain ignorant of the material available in these libraries. The lack of a proper trained staff keeps the Librarians busy with the clerical works of the library when the managerial and the organizational activities of the libraries need to be attended to. This is one of the sure proofs that the development of the college libraries do not meet the demands of time.

One more factor that stands responsible for the unbalanced growth of the college libraries is the expansion of the institutions for Higher Education. In this context the stress is often laid on increasing the collections of the college libraries and on the construction of separate library buildings, but very little provision or rather no provision whatsoever is made to strengthen the functional level of the libraries. No efforts are made either, to provide the library management with a well-qualified staff so that the libraries could work more efficiently. All these handicaps have defeated the very purpose of grants for books when there is no proper staff to process them and make them available to the users.

Contribution of Dr. S.R. Ranganathan

The libraries of the early 19th century made rapid progress due to the guidance of Dr. Ranganathan. During the pre-independence period, Ranganathan played a giant role in the Library Movement of the country, when libraries were regarded as insignificant except for a second position in Education. This great Mathematician and a great Scientist of the time, was the first great Librarian in the country.

An extract in Dr. Ranganathan's book on *College and School Libraries*, published in 1942, has created a great impact on the Library Movement in the country. He writes :

> "There is no disputing the fact that a very large portion of colleges in the country have no proper libraries, nor library buildings, to enable a first rate library service."

Over half a century ago, Dr. Ranganathan had already drawn up for us a picture of the college libraries, when he said :

> "College libraries consisted of closed cupboards. Most of them were concentrated in one or two rooms called the General Library. Hardly any student cared to go to this general library. A student could at best reach up to the barrier, select all by himself a title from a tattered-volume of printed catalogue and drop an application for it into a tray one morning each week. By the evening, the available books would all stand piled up on the desk. A lucky student might find his book in the pile, but he would often feel disappointed by the book not suiting his standard or by its being something different from what he thought it to be."

We are not far from this picture even to this day in many of our ill-equipped modern libraries in the country. Every library activity or service should co-relate to the classroom activity. But usually college education is centred round text-books. The main aim of the students with this sort of education is to finish the University examination and not to excel in knowledge. With this aim in view, notes become the object of study and rarely even the prescribed books are read. With the result, reference books are never consulted. If libraries are visited at all, it is only for lighter recreational reading.

From the 19th to 20th century, we owe much of the progress of libraries in the country, to the untiring efforts of Dr. S.R. Ranganathan and after him to Professor P.N. Kaula, who is looked upon as 'The Second to None' in the library profession today. Besides these two great Giants, there have been a few others who have been playing the important role of Leadership in the Library Profession. We must admit that the speed of this progress has no doubt slowed down with the death of Ranganathan. On the other hand, we can be proud that Professor P.N. Kaula who is on the library scene with his untiring efforts for the growth of the library profession and of the library movement in the country. He has kept the library profession still alive and active and has given a promise of a bright hope for its future development.

It was in 1928, that Dr. S.R. Ranganathan started the first library training programme for the college Librarians at Delhi. This pattern was soon followed by the Benaras Hindu University, and thereafter, it developed widely in many other States of the country. As years went by, the library training drifted from its original motivation making the vision of library service deemed. Libraries to be Service-oriented, requires a strong motivation for a practical use of skills to disseminate knowledge. In spite of several drawbacks, the library service has somehow come to its rightful place in meeting the demands of the community which it serves.

Dr. Ranganathan, by his dedication to the library profession, has left us a rich legacy through his original contributions, innovative ideas and new knowledge, to endow the Library Science with a content and meaning that could meet the challenges of all times in information handling and library service. Ranganathan has been rightly described as the "Father of the Library Movement in India". He has also been instrumental in introducing the library legislation (which has been accepted in six States so far).

The Fifth Law of Library Science focuses on the growing aspect of the library. Ranganathan could presume even as early as in 1930, that with the advent of a 'paperless society', library as a physical artifact could disappear, but that the role of professional Informational Specialists would not undergo much change. Infact, he presummed that the printed book would itself be replaced in the transmission of information.

If Dr. Ranganathan were here in our midst this day, surely the College and University Libraries would be able to receive much encouragement to meet the changing needs of Higher Education in the modern society and of the individual. He would also require of the Librarians, that they give a serious thought to all the aspects of the implications of electronic publishing for the library profession. He would undoubtedly urge them to remember the Fifth Law of Library Science, the observance of which becomes more vital at present than it was fifty or sixty years ago. The modern Librarianship would find through the Leadership of Ranganathan a way to go forward. Herein lies the greatness of Ranganathan.

In his Mootham Report of 1953, Ranganathan had also recommended that the library finance must be voted for liberally with a generosity and a vision of its future growth. Today, this vision seems to have drifted far away from the actual scene where College and University Libraries are concerned.

It was the hard work of Dr. Ranganathan, his painstaking efforts and his spirit of dedication, that made his endeavour to make India, a library conscious country. Through his works and his professional Leadership, he did prepare the ground for the changes that would be brought about in academic libraries in the years to come.

4

Assessment and Evaluation of Individual College Library

In the State of Bihar there are eight Universities and about 400 colleges. Except for a few, most of the colleges and University libraries are poorly managed with no proper funds and no proper qualified library staff. The documents on the shelf are often out of date and do not meet the requirements of students and teachers. These libraries have no adequate provision for study or for leisure reading. The documents on shelves are un-cared for and no trouble is taken to have orderly arrangement on shelves. Such a state does not facilitate the readers to search for the material of their requirement.

A few college libraries that came under the survey of the author in the Capital of Bihar are :

(1) B.N. College Library
(2) Patna College Library *
(3) Science College Library *
(4) Bihar College of Engineering Library
(5) Magadh Mahila College Library
(6) Patna Women's College Library
(7) Patna Medical College Library

The main part of the survey of the college libraries in the State included a detailed Assessment and Evaluation of a model college library. It is the Women's College Library, with a Lady Librarian at its helm. The present library building of Patna Women's College Library is raised with the U.G.C. grants. It is a spacious library for a college where the students enjoy many facilities although with a minimum staff.

The Patna Women's College library dates back to the foundation of the college in 1940. The library was started with about 300 books borrowed from a local institution for the use of its students. In the course of years and with the availability of funds, a few books were purchased and the borrowed books returned to the shelves where they belonged. With the growth of the college, the library also grew and was managed by one of the teachers. The old Register System for recording and issuing of books was now followed. This small library was housed in one of the classrooms of the college. During the years that followed, the library began to shift from one room to another larger one until 1980.

In 1981 the classroom library was shifted to its proper building with a trained Lady Librarian to manage and organize its activities. It took three years to equip and to furnish this new block and it kept struggling for qualified staff for better efficiency. It is an accepted fact that Patna Women's College, a Constituent College of the Patna University, is one of its best colleges, and as such, the college library too shares this status despite its small-sized staff of eight members. There is now a constant request to extend its floor space and its services for longer hours. The present existing staff cannot meet the increasing demands of the increasing number of students. There is a rush at every section of the library especially during the peak hours of the day. The functions of this library are divided into several sections to render efficient, effective and profitable services to its student community.

1. **The Acquisition Section** (Includes Book Selection) :

The yearly book purchases are made by the subject experts of the college in consultation with the Librarians so as to avoid duplication of reading materials. The purchasing committee which is made up of one teacher from each department, meets once a year to discuss the needs of the students. It draws up lists of reading materials which are scrutinized by the library staff.

The selection of books is one of the difficult problems in the proper functioning of the libraries. Realizing the lack of sound scientific basis for selection of books, Dr. S.R. Ranganathan had observed :

> "Booksellers often contact the Principals or the Heads of the Departments and they try to tempt them in getting such books selected as would decrease the quality and utility of the book collection in the library. During the busy academic engagements, the teachers fail to verify the up-to-dateness of the book. The result is, that out-moded and unwanted books often enter into the libraries."

The Librarian has very little choice in selecting the needed books for the library. Neither the Publishers' catalogues are consulted nor are the needs of the readers in the library taken into consideration by the teachers. Hence, 90 per cent of selected books remain unused on the shelves in the library.

A well-equipped and a well-managed library is the foundation of modern educational structure. Library as an Information Centre has to collect, process store and retrieve the right kind of information at the right time and to the right user. Book selection is often understood to be as the function of choosing reading materials. Rather, in Book Selection, the central function of the library is to build and to develop the library collections so as to enable the library to organize its reading materials which furthers the objective of the particular library. Hence proper skills for book selection have to be acquired by getting familiar with books and bibliographies. Selection and acquisition is an important part of the library works and needs care, intelligence and good judgement. Both, the book selection and acquisition must be based on the objects of the library. The frequency of selection and of acquisition must be continuous.

Book selection needs evaluation and this is done by a personal inspection and by reading the Book Reviews. The Book Reviews are found in Scientific and Technical Periodicals, and Weekly additions of Newspapers. Book Reviews is the best tool for book evaluation. It includes reviews and criticisms of new books. There are five categories for reviewing publications, namely, the Blurb, Newspapers, Dailies with Review Columns, general magazines with the review columns, subject periodicals with review articles and journals which have no feature articles. Book Reviews analyses the merits and demerits of the book and state which readers would appreciate the particular books.

The Librarians at Patna Women's College enjoy the freedom to make purchases of special reference material to enrich the library collections. The purchase of books is limited to the minimum funds received each Year and which keeps on increasing and decreasing every year (Table 4.1).

To encourage reading and book buying habits, the library, catalogues the addresses of both Indian and Foreign Publishing Houses, which would serve as Ready Reckoners for the purchase of text and reference books as well as other interesting reading materials. In the long run this service would help in changing the quality of the annual and departmental purchases, which as of now tend to be hurried or un-informed or determined by the local availability factor.

TABLE 4.1 Book Grants Received by the College Library

(Rs.)

Source	1987-88	1988-89	1989-90	1990-91	1991-92
Patna University P.G. (Home Sc.)	10,000	10,000	–	–	–
University Grants Commission Yearly grants	25,000	2,40,000	–	85,000	1,57,500
State Govt. Grants	–	–	–	–	–
By Gifts and Donations	74	1167	1,200	39	154
Total	35,074	2,51,167	1,200	85,039	1,57,654

Notes :

- .The yearly grants for P.G. (H.Sc.) from Patna University was received for 1987-88 and 1988-89 only.
- No grants have been received from the Patna University by the college library for the years 1987-88 onwards due to financial crises in the State of Bihar.
- Gifts/Donations are made in kind by students, teachers and friends of the college. They are put in money-value for the sake of statistics. The donated books become useful for the use of the library readers and borrowers.
- No UGC grant was received during the year 1989-90.

What is important is, that information services be planned with an eye on current areas of interest to the students and the teaching community-ranging from radio listening to music – in short, the Tracking Clubs. The interesting students can be fruitfully involved in adding to the scope and repertoire of library information on services and collections. Dissemination of information would thus go a long way in changing stereotypical attitude towards libraries among students, teacher, librarians, education planners and founders.

2. Cataloguing and Classification Section

The catalogue cards are filed in the catalogue cabinets according to subject and author sequence. The arrangement of cards is modified to suit the use of the students of the college. The library also maintains the Shelf-List.

The classification system followed at present is the Dewey Decimal System, although there is a plan to allow Colon Classification System at least in some of the subjects in the near future. The DDC System has been followed from the start and is more convenient.

TABEL 4.2 : Statistics pertaining to the use of Reference Books

Subject	1987-88	1988-89	1989-90	1990-91	1991-92
Philosophy	3292	1762	1388	1111	2143
Psychology	6401	2553	2856	1959	2978
Political Science	906	5749	4510	4309	5940
Economics	12215	7902	7463	3724	8140
Sociology	8482	4110	3119	2221	2321
Languages	511	195	133	60	79
Science & Maths	668	929	1287	717	1457
Home Science	4636	3140	2282	1325	2126
Literature	8224	7128	4704	4398	5681
History	16436	8139	5840	4423	6475
Geography	3613	3639	4883	3698	3290
P.G. (Home Science)	1933	1991	1710	878	511
General Reading	56	126	136	99	143
Fiction	157	51	109	110	118
Total	67530	47414	40420	29032	41402

Note : Statistics for the year 1990-91 could hardly be taken into account due to various disturbances in the running of the academic session. The library too suffered where normal services were concerned.

3. The Reference Section

This is the busiest section of the day when about two hundred students per period use the reference section for reference work every day. Open access system is followed here with a strict vigilance. Inspite of it, the mutilation and other malpractices do take place from time to time. Such cases, when detected, are dealt with accordingly. About five to six books get written off in this section every year.

The daily statistics of the use of reference books is carefully maintained (Table 4.2). The reference books cover up all the subjects taught in the college. Besides, the other general reference books, like the encyclopaedias in social sciences, philosophy and other subject encyclopaedias, a variety of dictionaries, year books, handbooks, annals, directories and so on, are very much used by the students to increase their knowledge in various subjects. Fiction and other volumes of Biographies of Great Men like Jawaharlal Nehru, Gandhiji, Vivekananda and so on, are also available in this section. This enables the students to cultivate a love and interest for reading. Books on painting, arts, rare books and pictorial Atlases add to the number of reference books in the section. The services of the Library staff in this section are very much appreciated and valued by the students. Silence in the section as well as in every part of the library is maintained very rigidly. This was admittedly resisted in the earlier years. But the insistence has paid off. However, the statistics have been uneven from year to year due to the strikes and other disturbances which has caused the library to function in an irregular manner.

4. The Periodical Section

During the peak hour of the day, this section is rather crowded. About 200 students visit the section daily. This adds up to about 6,000 readers per month and about 72,000 readers per year. More readers cannot be accommodated here due to the limited space. The section displays journals on subjects such as, economics, history, political science, home science, mathematics, philosophy, science and technology, sports, films and other popular magazines in various languages besides English, taught in the classrooms, like Hindi, Bengali, Urdu and Maithili. Lighter reading materials, magazines on general knowledge, aptitude tests, etc., are also displayed (Table 4.3). The library does not receive any separate fund for the upkeep of this section. The expenditure for the purchase of the lighter reading material and the magazine is paid from the created fund in the library. The out-dated periodicals are preserved for three years. After that some useful periodicals are bound, others are destroyed or sold as junk after the useful clippings are cut out if any.

TABLE 4.3 : **A** : Records of Journal (current and bound) **B** : Expenditure statement on Journals and Newspapers

	Journals:	1987-88	1988-89	1989-90	1990-91	1991-92
A:	Current:	1000	1005	1008	1005	1025
	Bound :	122	–	130	37	209
	Total	1122	1005	1138	1042	1234
		Rs.	Rs.	Rs.	Rs.	Rs.
B:	Periodicals:	4,126	6,007	4,000	14,000	30,229
	Newspapers:	2,019	800	300	150	2,000
	Total	6,145	6,807	4,300	14,150	32,229

Note: 1. Figures for bound periodicals during 1988-89 are nil due to financial crisis.

2. Due to the financial crisis and disturbances in the proper functioning of colleges and libraries, the number of periodicals and newspapers had to be reduced. In the case of newspapers the receiving number was cut down as there were no students visiting the library in a normal way.

5. The Newspaper Section

This section is well used by the staff and students of the college throughout the day. The section is maintained by funds created in the library. The newspapers are preserved for one year for want of space. At the end of the year, useful clippings are cut out and placed in the clipping files item-wise for the use of research scholars.

The headlines of the newspapers are high-lighted on the board at the entrance to the library. This is a great help for students to pick up the important news for the day at a glance especially when they are pressed for time. The newspapers subscribed by the library are the local and national dailies in English, Hindi, Urdu and Maithili.

The newspaper section also maintains the Clippings Files. This is a laborious work especially without a separate staff to manage the sectional work. The important news items are clipped together. From time to time, these are sorted out. Each clipping is then mounted on a sheet of paper, recording the name of the newspaper and the date. Each mounted sheet of paper is then sealed, classified and signed by one in charge of the section. Finally the clippings of each category are put together to be bound in book-form for use as social service research materials for research scholars.

6. **The Audio Section**

The college students spend their free time in this section. At present the section maintains one tape recorder with French and TOFEL cassettes of three months and two weeks learning duration respectively. The help books for language learning for students planning to study overseas contain the features for speech-training. There is a plan in the near future to have at least one TV set with ear-phones in the section. Besides the language learning cassettes, the section has also other musical cassettes, the *ragas* of morning and evening prayers, speech cassettes of great and learned men and women like Gandhiji, Nehruji, Mrs. Indira Gandhi and so on. The section besides being used for learning, serves also a place for relaxing.

The section contains books on film-making, film-direction, film-acting and film-reviews. The possibilities in this direction hardly needs to be emphasized, if it is recognized, that films are one of the most important media of social communication, education and all round development of the youth. Films have the ability to evoke authentic tone of societies.

The students as well as adults, love to see films of books they have read especially the most famous ones like "French Lieutenant's Woman" or "Passage to India". At times a film is spoken of as, a "Book" or a "Film" is also spoken of as, "Story". Our Indian films have yet to enter into this idealized vision and thus reach the golden age when it will make its task to interpret the modern world to the common man to discuss the shape of things to come and open up ways brought about by the advancement of science.

Information today is no longer confined to the traditional printed form, but Audio Visual and visual materials are the new information carriers and films in particular are important modes of communication, entertainment and education. The Maharaja Sayajirao Gaekward of the Princely State of Baroda had shown an interest in this medium as early as in 1911. Later, in 1973, the British Government made its initial efforts to introduce Audio-Visual Education as part of the post-war educational Development Plan. Ever since then, efforts are being made to develop the use of films at the level of academic education and gradually it has been given importance at the level of Higher Education. The Film Library Movement unfortunately has not yet really picked up.

The Education in the country has not yet geared towards this movement. The Central Film Library, the department of Teaching Aids (DTA) and the NCERT, Delhi, is the Apex Body for Educational films not only for India, but for all the South Asian countries as well. The Central Film Library (CFL) offers loan facilities to all Educational institutions for various vocational activity.

Films cover various areas in Education both at the College and University levels. A variety of subjects, like, history, literature, arts, science, social education, etc., and also the various regional languages can be taught through the medium of films both in Hindi and in English. The UGC Scheme to open Film Clubs in colleges and Universities, could be yet another starting point to add to the library collections.

7. Women's Study Section

This section, is needless to say, important considering the proliferation of women's study Centres and the status of Women. The section has acquired resource papers, journals from activitists Women's Organizations, as also catalogues of publications prepared by advance Centres of Women's Studies, Journals, like *Manushi* add to the literature on Women's Studies. Exposure to this section goes a long way in providing the much needed perspective among the readers.

8. Academic Information Section

It displays the various information magazines and pamphlets and notices regarding scholarship awards available for students to enter into Higher Studies, job avenues or travel allowances and guidance to those who wish to go abroad. It is a very informative section highly valued by staff and students of the college.

To build an academic information section is a great potential in all academic libraries. To make this section effective, one must be well-versed in the availability of academic and vocational courses. For this purpose, an Academic File has to be maintained under various information needs. For example : information relating to Fellowship and scholarships offered by UGC, ICSSR, ICMR, and others will be systematically arranged for the use of the faculty members as well as for students.

Likewise, information abstracts of major forth coming seminars and conferences organized by various academic disciplines, like the ICSSR, ICS, and others. This sort of information can be very enriching to increase knowledge in any particular subject.

There are also scholarships and awards available, such as :

- Tourism
- IGNOU
- Commonwealth Scholarships
- FCO Scholarships and Awards
- INLAKS Scholarships
- Research Awards
- Bihar

also finds its place in this section for the benefit of the students. For students not intending to persue Higher Education, the section offers Information Abstracts on Vocational Courses like : 'MIT's Dual Qualification Scheme.' which offers exciting computer courses. Today we have many more modern Computer Courses like, Apple, NIIT, LCC, APTECH, UCL, HCL and so on.

9. The Circulation Section

The Circulation Section is the most important and the busiest section in the library. The daily issue statistics (Table 4.4) are strictly maintained and totalled every month and shown in the yearly records. Table 4.4 shows very high number of issues during 1991-92 compared with other years. The fluctuating totals are dependent on the regular and irregular academic year.

The circulation counter follows the Brown's System for issuing and returning of books. The Asstt. Librarians and two peons work at this section. Books are applied for through slips as no open access is yet possible in the stack for want of personnel.

The other sections are : The Book Bank Section which lends books to about 100 poor and deserving students on payment of a deposit of Rs. 20 only as caution fee for the year. The Xeroxing Section started since 1988. It helps to eliminate destruction of reading materials. The students profit greatly from this library facility. It is a time-saving device both for the library and for the students. The Rare Book Section is under closed access. These books are issued for use on request only. The section contains valuable reference books, pictorial books such as Great Ages of Man, Needlework and Cookery, Gardening, Architecture, Home Planning and other similar material.

TABLE 4.4 : Statistics of the Circulation Section

Subjects	1987-88	1988-89	1989-90	1990-91	1991-92
Philosophy	951	719	1188	902	922
Psychology	1082	1172	1769	1003	1807
Sociology	1431	672	1782	1374	1492
Political Science	2170	1522	2538	1736	2913
Economics	3027	244	2429	2022	3741
Languages	54	124	328	328	1001
Science and Maths	510	513	1847	687	2022
Home Science	929	1042	1722	911	1286
Literature	1233	1175	2633	1580	3511
History	2551	1869	2876	2115	2107
Geography	458	642	1321	1016	2087
P.G. (Home Sc.)	276	484	964	648	921
Fiction	222	158	608	287	697
General Reading	37	21	232	353	41
Total	14931	12557	22237	14962	25548

Note: The above statistics are collected daily at the end of the day and added up every month to get the yearly total.

Due to rise in prices, the books added every year to the library collections depends on the grants received (Table 4.5). The total collection at present is over 74,000 volumes. It has in its holdings about 80 historical, political and geographical maps which are well used by the respective teachers. The generous donations of books has helped much to increase the holdings in the library.

The library is further strengthened and guided in its organizational works by the library committee. The Committee meets twice in the year to evaluate the various activities of the library and to take decisions and to make further plans for its developments. Much of the growth and progress of the library is due to the strong support the Librarian receives from the members of the Library Committee.

The yearly activities of the library are a source of learning for college staff and students. These have helped the staff to change and to develop their teaching methods. These activities comprise of Book Exhibitions, Book Talks, Display, Quizes, Symposias, Library Week and the like. At the beginning of every academic year, orientation talks are conducted by the Librarian herself for the freshers to help them to know the library. Practical demonstration to other older students is held to create an awareness of what the library should mean to them if they are to profit from its services.

Table 4.5 : Yearly Additions to the Library Holdings

Sections	1987-88	1988-89	1989-90	1990-91	1991-92
General Section	1019	10941	503	938	521
Book Bank Section	131	154	91	294	98
P.G. (Home Science) Section	229	20	40	162	–
Gifts & Donation Section	74	1167	1200	39	154
Total received each year	1453	12282	1834	1423	773

Notes. 1. During the two years, 1988-89 and 1989-90 the donated books were very high in number.
2. The year 1991-92 was declared to be the 0 (zero) year.

The system of organizing library funds and record-keeping was introduced when the library was shifted to the new block in 1981. It was only in 1984 when a suitable staff was appointed, could the library plan out its organizational works and create its own funds in order to self-finance the library for its efficient functioning.

The Qualifications of the Staff are as follows:

Librarian : Trained B.Lib. & Inf. Sc. (Degree Course)
Asstt. Librarian : Trained B. Lib.Sc. (Degree Course)
Library Assistant : Semi-trained (Diploma Course)
Typist : Certificate Course
Sorter : Lib. Sc. (one month-Certf. course)
Mechanic : Certificate in electrification

Peon : Matric certificate.

Patna Women's College
Library Staff

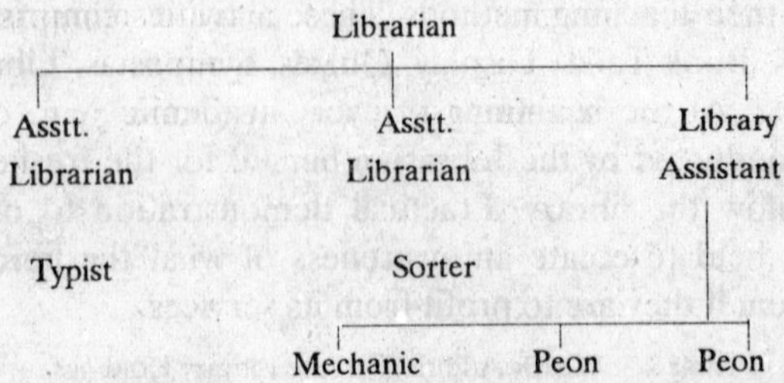

The library staff at Patna Women's College is however paid by the Patna University Office through the College Office in the pay-scales as per Table 4.6. All regular appointments are made and approved by the University authorities through the Bihar Government after being advertised by the Bihar State Service Commission.

TABLE 4.6 : Statement of Salaries paid to the Library Staff as in 1993

Sl. No.	Designation	Scale of Pay
1.	Librarian (trained)	2000-60-2300-75-3200-100-3500
2.	Asstt. Librarian (trained)	- do-
3.	Library Asstt. (semi-trained)	- do -
4.	Library Typist (certificate holder)	1300-30-1560-40-2040
5.	Technician (trained)	775-12-955-14-1025
6.	Peon (Matric)	- do -
7.	Peon (Matric) working as Sorter	- do -

Due to the financial crisis in the State of Bihar the monthly salaries are not paid timely. Hence, the employees' constant strickes for timely payment of salaries due to them, paralyses the working of the whole library several times during the academic year.

Apart from grants sanctioned for purchase of books, all other items of expenditure are incurred from the amounts collected through the creation of funds by the library. A detailed account of income and expenditure is given in Table 4.7 for the financial year 1991-92.

TABLE 4.7 : Balance Sheet of Income and Expenditure for two years only
Financial year : 1991-92 and 1992-93

	Income			Expenditure	
	1991-92	1992-93		1991-92	1992-93
Lib. Fee	40,060.00	18816.00	Mag. & N. Papers	10000	8356.26
Lib. Fund	3,105.95	20259.00	Binding	4228	10,000.00
Caut. Deposit	1,045.00	895.00	Equip.	20000	–
Printing	7,201.00	5650.00	Gen. Rep.	2416	8558.58
Xeroxing	22,531.45	19463.40	Printing	510	12241.00
Misc.	847.55	1087.40	Caut. Refund	1675	5375.00
			Xeroxing	4645	397.30
			Misc.	21295.19	13785.88
Total	74,790.95	66,170.80	Total:	64,769.19	58714.02
Solicitated amount:	10,021.76	7,456.78			
Grand Total	64,769.19	58,714.02		64,769.19	58714.02

Note: 1. The Balance sheet of the college library is drawn up every year.
2. As the academic year is irregular, there is an irregularity in income and expenditure of the year.

Due to the irregularity of grants the expenditure could not be incurred fully of the amounts availed hence ear marked balances remained to be carried over for the next financial year.

The Patna Women's College Library in the State of Bihar thus fulfils the demands put on a modern library to help readers and potential users step into the world of learning. It could be regarded as a Model Library to all college libraries within the State in its functional and organizational system. The UGC Team who visited the college libraries and after checking the working of the several libraries in the year 1989 had this remark to make:

> "The Patna Women's College Library is of APPRECIATIVE EXCELLENCE. It is a model library for all the college libraries. It has an excellent functioning system. The library is well used and much appreciated by all the students and staff of the college. A library of this kind should be kept open for longer hours. It is indeed a library of appreciative excellence."

However, the library is facing many difficulties due to inadequate staff, absence of Refresher courses for the staff, inadequate funds and lack of space. It is about time that college Librarians tied up with the teachers' movement to campaign for more meaningful fund allocations without which planning and equipment for the future will be near impossible task.

5

Standardization in College Libraries

Role, Need and Purpose of Standards

Standards, norms and guidelines are required for organizing library work, and for quick retrieval of information. There is need of a Standard Scheme for classification and of a standard Code for the work of cataloguing.

Standardization is used in libraries today, to speed up library work and to disseminate information which is both manual and mechanical. The purpose of standardization in larger libraries is to advance its services to the users. Standards also help in the work of organization and arrangement of information and documents in its collection.

Due to information explosion, users have specific demands. The advances in information technology have helped to solved to a large extent, the problem of retrieving information, from a vast amount of useful literature. In this context, library functions have been changing over the past few decades. Hence, there is need to further develop the existing Indian Standards and to formulate new ones.

The concept of college library and its services has been changing since the beginning of the 20th century in almost every country. In India, this change has not yet taken a correct perspective. Over the past few years, several Commissions and Committees have well stated that libraries and their activities must influence all other Educational activities and academic institutions. Surveys of many of the academic libraries in the State of Bihar and in some other parts of the country show that the libraries are far from being satisfactory.

Although there have been enormous efforts on the part of the Authorities in the field of development of the libraries, the advancement of Higher Education, has not yet gained the necessary importance. The functioning of a well equipped academic library has not yet come to be considered as a vital part of the process of academic education. Unlike the libraries of the past, the modern libraries are to a certain extent, powerful Educational forces in the society. At the same time, the large resources in these libraries meet with problems when information has to be retrieved and disseminated. This is surely due to the lack of proper norms, guidelines or standards. Lack of proper standards leads to waste of expenditure in acquisition, processing and dissemination of information.

Stock Logistics is yet another Standard today applied in modern libraries (Fig. 5.1). Although it is an ancient technic, the concept of logistic management entails, planning, directing, controlling and organizing within a time-frame, and which is a specific function.

The concept of logistics dates back to antiquity. LOGISTICS is a Greek name which means "*SKILLED in Calculation*". During the Roman and Byzantine time, the word LOGISTA meant "administrative official". The term organization has two inter-related meanings. Organization can be viewed as an structure or an organization can be a process of arranging or structuring parts of an organization, in such a systematic manner so that the functional activities are grouped together. To this concept and task of organization, fundamental logic could be applied. Thus a simple organizational structure for the library could be as follows:

(1) Organizing Structure
(2) Distribution of library man-power
(3) Adoption of new technology
(4) Acceptance of both the user and the provider.

Further a tactical approach to Logistics would mean:

(a) *Macro-level logistics* which involves a individual business relationship of the suppliers, publishers and vendors. This relationship can be either within the country or abroad. The aspect of this approach would extend to:

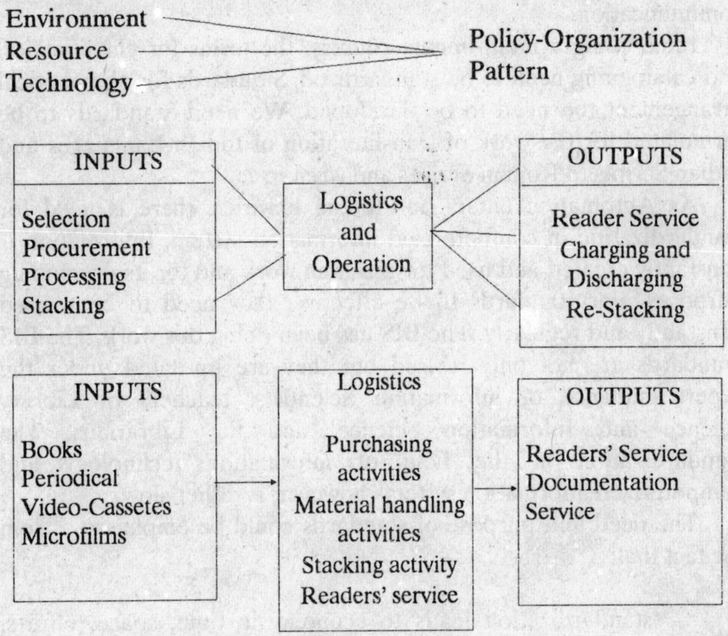

Fig. 5.1. A Chart of Stock Logistics

– Economic environment
– Geo-political
– Legal aspect

(b) *Micro-level logistics*: Here the library activities can be divided as follows:

– Procurement and processing
– Stacking, binding, rectifying
– Reader Services.

Modern day terms – logistics, physical distribution and logistic management are assumed to be synonymous and are therefore interchangeable. These terms are intra-organizational activities which form a total system of purchase, inventory control, handling transportation, warehousing, site location, order processing, man-power distribution, organizational structuring and communication.

India being a multi-lingual country, the terms for classification and cataloguing need to be standardized. Standards for alphabetical arrangement too need to be developed. We need Standards to be formulated for the work of transliteration of Indian Languages and Indian Scripts to Roman Scripts and *vice versa*.

As Automation enters our Indian libraries, there is need for standardization in computerized information system. Information is constantly created and used for research work and for its developing purposes. For standards to be effective, they need to be revised constantly and regularly. The BIS has been doing this work. The BIS Standards are not only revised but they are up-dated under the expert guidance of information Scientists, teachers of Library Science and Information Science, and the Librarians. The standardization in the field of information technology and computerized information systems however, is rather slow.

The need and purpose of standards could be emphasized from the fact that:

- standardization leads to economy in time, space, efforts, materials, manpower and money.
- they act as a tool for exchange and for transfer of information.
- they act as a tool of measurement and control the quality of service and collection.
- they act as innovation, making the libraries to be efficient Agents of service, and
- they help in saving time and effort in the routine works of the library.

Standards then could be developed, formulated and applied to compilation work and for the re-packaging of information. When they are applied to secondary and tertiary sources of information, we have the products of tertiary, of indexing and of abstracting sources as well as services.

Present Service Aspect in College Libraries

A short survey conducted of a few academic libraries in Bihar, has revealed facts regarding the collections, services and use of library materials.

In most of the academic institutions, students hardly visit the library as they remain closed during most of the working hours. Besides, there is no facility provided for reading and reference work. In some cases, the libraries were made use of with a view to score high marks at examinations, rather, than to gain knowledge. With the result, only those books which covered the examination study were being used. The rest of the material remained untouched and even unknown to the students.

Very few college libraries had library committees. Those which did have, proved to be inactive and without any incentive for further development of libraries or library resources. No college or school library had any book selection policy. The books are purchased almost overnight in order to spend the sanctioned grant. The students have no say in the matter and their requirements are not considered at all. Often the books are purchased to suit the needs of the teachers and not so much the needs of the students. The purchases are more quantitative rather than qualitative.

Funds in general were found inadequate compared with the rising prices of books. The libraries received no funds for building repairs nor for the development of the library. The Librarians have no provision to create funds from the library fee.

Many of the students complained of the low standard of collections in the library holdings and most of them were not satisfied with the library services rendered to them. Majority of the students looked forward to the time when the libraries would remain open for longer hours with more staff to serve their needs.

To solve all these problems and to make our libraries more efficient, there is need of Standards to be formulated. There should be standards for library functions, library services, for budget planning, staff appointments, inter-loan services, for organizational and administrative works as well.

Standardization

To have a standard is to measure an activity by judging its authenticity. A standard applies to any principle or a measure used to determine a quantity, value or quality of anything. There are two kinds of Standards for library work and services. The "Diagnostic" and "Projective" Standards. The diagnostic standard is based on a model of the conditions prevailing in the best of the libraries; while the projective standard is independent of the situation prevailing in the existing libraries. This is an ideal standard but it is not a reality. It is however, important as it standard but it is not a reality. It is however, important as it underlines the major achievements. But, both these standards, namely, the diagnostic and the projective standards, are necessary and can be combined in libraries on the model of the best existing library.

Besides these two standards, we have the "Productive" or "Job" Standards. Both of these standards are useful for specific areas of work in the libraries. Based on these standards, some guidelines could be drawn up for the working of our various libraries.

We also have the ISI Standard formulated for Documentation. These standards relate to library work, library buildings, equipment, furniture and fittings.

Originally, standardization was done only for commodities. Today, Standardization is used for all kinds of services and procedures. In libraries the technique of standards is very helpful both in the creative and in repetitive works. Were libraries are concerned, a library standard would provide criteria to judge the effectiveness of library work and services. A standard can be a measure for further development. It can be an instrument to take new decisions and new action by the librarian or by the authority for the improvement of the functions of library services or library work.

Standards serve as guidelines or as directives for the Librarian and the Library Staff in their work. We may say that standards are more for theoretical work and are more rigid, while guidelines reflect more on the practical way of running a library. Standardization is a unit which can be applied to libraries in their various operations, such as, collection development, staff appointments, organizational works, library services, budget and administration.

Standards relate not only to library works but also to location of libraries, staff, collections and services keeping them within the framework and thus making the libraries as efficient Agents of social change.

Location of Libraries

(1) Centrally located library would be accessible to a larger number of readers.

(2) A proper location is a must with the possibility of proper expansion
(3) The library building facing the Northern side receives the maximum light.
(4) A separate entrance to the library would be of great help.
(5) The library building should be spacious with sufficient equipment.
(6) The reference and magazine sections should be equipped with comfortable and relaxing furniture.

Library services

(1) The reference section should be provided with reference books pertaining to each subject.
(2) There should be at least ten learned periodicals in a subject for conducting teaching programmes.
(3) There should be at least ten copies of each prescribed book for the use of students.
(4) Audio Visual Aids could be supplemented for effective teaching programmes.
(5) A steady supply of maximum reading material would certainly broaden the vision of students, resulting in self-study and research.

Other Library Services

(1) The library should within its area have the facility for Inter-Loan Service code and resource sharing.
(2) Orientation courses/lectures should be arranged to enable the fresher for a better use of the library.

General Library Services

(1) Services of a trained librarian be employed when the library is open for longer hours.
(2) A balanced collection be built up of books, journals, and non-book materials.
(3) Readers be encouraged to use the library tools and other reading materials in the library.
(4) The library should remain open at least for eight to twelve

hours with a shift system.

(5) The library should have an open access system.

(6) Books be written off during the year as per UGC norms.

(7) The library should remain open throughout the year except on public holidays.

(8) A library committee should be constituted which should be advisory in nature.

(9) Up to date techniques in classification and cataloguing be used in order to organize and to retrieve documents.

(10) There should be automated services to quicken the retrieval and dissemination of information.

Library staff

(1) A well equipped library should have a professional staff with adequate training, ability and salary.

(2) A Staff Formula be drawn up in every library.

(3) For college libraries, the staff should comprise of the following:
   (i) Nine Professionals
   (ii) Nine semi-professionals including sorters and peons.

Library Collection

(1) The latest editions in literature and other subjects should up-date the collections of the library.

(2) Facilities of Book Banks should be provided for at least 50 per cent students of the weaker sections of the society.

(3) A uniform policy be drawn up for building up the library collection.

Library Finance

(1) At least 6 to 7 per cent of the college budget be allotted for library expenditure.

(2) Book Grants be made available at the beginning of each session.

(3) The utilisation of library grant to be planned during each financial year.

The Librarian

(1) The Librarian should be responsible for the overall organization of the library.
(2) The Librarian should be directly responsible to the Principal of the college/Head of the institution.
(3) It is the duty of the librarian to supervise the staff in the acquisition of reading materials.
(4) The Librarian should encourage the readers in the use of reference materials.

Such norms as above would help to enthuse in the readers the need for intellectual growth during the period of their study. A library would then be a place where idle minds would be changed to research-oriented minds. These minds would be imbued with a desire to satisfy their curiosity for more and more knowledge.

Standardization in India

In India, the importance of standardization was brought out in 1958. It was at this time that ISI Committee revised and finalised fifty eight standards. The area covered by these standards are:

- Bibliographical references
- Books and Periodicals
- Indexes and Abstracts
- Classification and Cataloguing
- Building
- Furniture and fittings
- Microflims

Standardization in India came to be formulated as early as in 1952. Some of these early standards are recorded below:

1952 : Guide for alphabetical arrangement
1976 : Guide for preparation of abstracts
1976 : Rules for making alphabetical Indexes
1988 : Guidelines for presentation of Information in technical manuals.

Other standards drawn up by BIS are:

1956 : Specification for author Statement in the Title Page of a book.

1974 : Guide for preparation and production of text books.

Standardization in our country has not yet reached the non-conventional documents in a total way. Some of the areas where standardization has reached are:

1966 : Code of practice for processing of microfilm
1967 : Guide for placement of images in roll microfilm
1980 : Guide for placement of images in roll microfilm

With the growth of literacy in India, there came also the growth and development of Education and the establishment of Universities and institutions of Higher Education. This enormous growth brought along with it certain amount of norms recommended through the education Commissions and Committees. Through these norms there came improvement in library collections and in library services. This gave a proper shape to the libraries in the country. A standard norm for budget as an annual grant for libraries was laid down at this time by the Radha Krishnan Commission. It also recommended a non-recurring grant every five years for the development of library collection.

Standardization in U.K. and U.S.A.

The following standards were drawn up in U.K. and in U.S.A. during the years 1959 and 1971 respectively:

U.S.A.-1950 : 50,000 volumes of college libraries.

Up to 600 every 200 additional number = 10,000 books.
5 per sent of total amount of budget for three professionals.

U.K. - 1971 : For colleges of technology
25,000 volumes for Degree work colleges
10,000 volumes for non-degree work colleges 2 to 3 per cent finance of the total budget

Space : 6,000 sq. ft. for reading room (Junior College)
18,000 sq.ft. for reading room (Regional College)
Student ratio : 1:5 in colleges
Reading Space : 25 sq. ft. for under-graduate class
35 sq. ft. for post-graduate class
Staff Ratio : 14 to 60 professionals and non-professionals.

Standards is a criterion to measure the utility of library service:

- it encourages international cooperation among libraries
- it helps to be aware of the activities in other library units.
- it lays minimum requirements for library efficiency to be dealt by Committee members and the authorities.
- it rationalizes the library working on scientific lines.
- it increases confidence of the public in library services.

Contribution of Dr. S.R. Ranganthan

Dr. Ranganathan in his report submitted to the UGC Commission in 1957, recommended Rs. 15 per Capita for every registered student and Rs. 200 per teacher as grant for the purchase of books for the library. It was also stated that this grant could be enhanced to meet the rising cost of books. The change would vary according to the development of each University and College in each of the States in the country.

The U.G.C. Library committee had also laid down certain standards in the form of Recommendations. In the Report of 1965 the recommendations related to the UGC Grant for the following:

- Book Selection and Book Purchase
- Promotion of reading habit
- Weeding and loss of books
- Library staff
- Buildings
- Furniture and Fittings

The story of Dr. Ranganathan between 1924-72 is the story of the Development of Indian Academic Libraries. He introduced many new services and set up many new standards in the field of Library and Information Science.

In 1929 Ranganathan changed the closed access system into an open access system. This was the first new service introduced by him in our libraries in India. In this way he brought the academic and other libraries to a stage of transition. By 1962 the impact of this open access system was so great, that it was followed even in some of the University libraries in India. The open access system has helped to bring the users and the library collections together, giving them the freedom to browse and to choose the right material to meet their needs.

Another standard introduced by Dr. Ranganathan, our great Leader and guide, was the importance of Reference Service. Because of its many benefits, this service grew very fast. Today, Reference Service forms a very important feature, especially in the larger libraries in the country.

The Bibliographical service was again another standard introduced by Ranganathan. Today its impact is greatly felt in University and Research Libraries.

Another important standard used in modern libraries is the standard of Statistical Science for library works. This standard too was brought about by Dr. Ranganathan who was a great Mathematician of the time. The Statistical standard today has been developed under the concept of liberality.

The Five Laws of Library Science themselves formulated in 1931 by Dr. S.R. Ranganathan form the guide-lines for library works and functions. They guide the functions in the organizational works of the library, such as, gangways, shelf guides, bay guides, etc. Over the years, these guides have helped the librarians to make the profession not only progressive but also challenging.

The importance and impact of the Laws of Library Science is still influencing our modern libraries. These Laws form the norms guiding the libraries to be effective instruments of social change.

When Dr. Ranganathan entered the library profession, there were hardly any set standards for libraries and their functions. Ranganathan experimented his ideas which were new and exciting, and, which he had learnt in the Western countries during his study and work experience in these libraries, (for the first time at the University Library at Madras.) Here Ranganathan drew up his own standards which were high and useful. It was after 1944 that the standards framed by Ranganathan developed and were introduced in other academic libraries.

As Chairman of the Documentation Committee of ISI during 1947-1966, Ranganathan published many standards for our Indian Academic Libraries which include the following:

- Practice of layout of library catalogue Code.
- Recommendations for Bibliographical Reference
- Practice of alphabetical arrangement
- Canons for making Abstracts
- Guide for layout of Learned Periodicals.

Standardization in the organization and in the arrangements of documents consists in the work of classification, cataloguing, furniture and storage devices. In this line constant revision has to be done and new standards formulated, because of growth and development of knowledge and the changing needs of the users. Some of these standards are:

- Glossary for classification : 1963
- Glossary for Cataloguing : 1966
- Metal shelving Racks : 1975 (adjustable type).

In conclusion we must remember, that no norms or guidelines can serve for all times. Standards, Norms and Guidelines have to be checked, revised and re-evaluated from time to time, so as to fit them in the changing conditions of the period of time. The changes in Standards occur due to new developments, increase of book and furniture prices and so on.

A College/University library can be used to improve educational standards, only if its presence can exert influence on the academic community. If library activities are scientifically organized to meet the needs of the classroom both for teachers and students, then libraries can influence the educational system.

In India, the first concrete step in standardization started with the committee under the chairmanship of Dr. S.R. Ranganathan for the development of libraries. The U.G.C. recommended the following standards in 1959:

(1) *Book Collection* : A collection of 1 to 3 lakhs for University library
A collection of 100 to 5000 for Departmental libraries
A collection of 5000 to 50,000 for College libraries

(2) *Finance :* Total per Capita
Rs. 50 per students
Rs. 200 per teacher and Research scholar

(3) *Staff Requirement* :

Acquisition : One person for every 6000 volumes yearly
Periodicals : One person for every 500 Periodicals yearly
Documentation : One person for every 1000 entries (card) prepared per year.
Reference Section : One Person for every 50 readers per day.
Circulation : One person for every 1500 hours of working
Maintenance : One person for every 6000 volumes for issuing
One person for every 500 volumes replacement per day
One person for every one lakh volumes in existence : (50,000)

(4) *Administration* : One accountant, one typist, one library Assistant

(5) *Supervisors* : One librarian, one Dy. librarian, one library assistant (no standards for grades)

(6) *Space* : 1/5 of total number of students and 1/10 of teachers in the institution (University)
1/5 of students and 1/10 of teachers (Colleges)

(7) *Stack Room* : Length 1.80 n plus 3.15 m
(n : rows)
(m : gangways)
Width - 3 metres width for gangways
2 metres racks with breadth (2 plus 1)
5 metres 2 × 2 × 1
10 metres 4 × 2 × 2

(8) (a) *Height of Racks* : Floor of ceiling 2.35n : 8ft.
(b) *capacity of Book Rack* : 700-750 volumes in a 2 metre

rack (space of 1 sq. m. : 150 books can be arranged)

Today very few acceptable standards exist with various authorities,

e.g. : 1 ft. is for seven books

This standard is maintained by the standard Guide published by A.J. Handbooks, for economics, 1970. For technology Institutions the same guide handbook recommends another standard,

e.g. : 3 ft for 15 books (Technology)

The U.G.C. Recommendation reviewed at the INSDOC seminar had the following standards:

10 to 25 books for classification per day
12 books for cataloguing per day
40 books for accessioning per day
350 cards to be filed per day

It is up to each library to choose the standard that suit the workings of the particular library system.

6

Historical Background of Public Libraries

In the Northern part of India libraries have existed in some form or the other form early times. The large collections of the early Hindu manuscripts at Nalanda, Taxila, Patliputra and at Vaishali, together with the libraries of the medieval Hindu period at Ujjain, Banaras, Tanjore and Kashmir, are good examples of the existence of ancient libraries in our country.

There has also been a lot of literature in these ancient libraries. But this literature has not been used for systematic study nor for research purposes. A lot of records on education and on ancient India has been discovered in these libraries. But, none of these records give any systematic information about libraries except for a few scattered references. Yet, the records stress that Public Libraries were an important part of the Educational System of that period.

During the medieval period, libraries were not only places of pride for the Turks, Afghans and the Moghuls, but they were also very important institutions. During this period, a Librarian was held in great esteem and was honoured with white robes of Royalty. The Moghul Period was also known for this library activities. But the aspect of Librarianship was altogether ignored. The kings of this age were accepted as men of great learning. They were the patronisers of great libraries and of literature. But none of them ever gave any thought for the development of libraries. The books written at this time gave no information about the use of libraries nor of its functions. Sometimes a mention would be made of libraries with reference to their origin. But there was no descriptive information to be had anywhere.

In U.K. and in U.S.A., the origin of Public Libraries and its services can be traced to the 19th century. But it is primarily a 20th century development. Coming to the libraries of modern India, we have the library movement in the real sense, in the first decade of the 19th century in the Princely state of Baroda. This was a pioneering attempt at Library Movement in India. The Maharaja Sayaji Rao Gaekward, the Ruler of the State of Baroda, being impressed by the services rendered by the libraries in the West, engaged the services of W.A. Borden, an American Librarian, for opening and organizing the Central Library and the other libraries in the state in 1910. This was the first awakening in the State and in India.

Very soon, the sparks of this awakening light undoubtedly found its way towards the South. The fiery sparks struck very powerfully the State of Andhra Pradesh in 1914. With the enthusiasm of its people for the Library Movement, the First Andhra Library Association came into existence. The works of this Association were headed by the untiring efforts of Mr. Iyyanki Venkata Ramanayya, the First Great Pioneer of the Library Movement, in India.

Iyyanki, a young lad of 19 years, entered the public life in 1907, later to be known as the "Architect of Public Library Movement". Iyyanki joined the Freedom Movement in order to create a consciousness about the greatness of India. This role indeed gave him a double opportunity when in 1914, as President of the Library Association, he tried to create also a Library Movement and library consciousness in the country. Iyyanki had a simple style of living. He began at this time to love the library and its works more than his own kit and kin. He had the capacity of winning over many a young people. Prior to independence, he visited many villages and convinced the youth of the need of libraries in the country.

In 1911, having put forth his best to start a library movement, Iyyanki was made the First Secretary of the Ram Mohan Free Library at Vijayawada. In 1914 he founded the Andhra Pradesh Association of Indian Public Library Movement. In 1919, he organized the All India Public Library Association at Madras. He was also made its First Secretary. At Vijayawada, Iyyanki established the "Saraswati Samrajyam" (The World Federation of Wisdom) to draw attention of Library Experts and Professionals and to extend the Library Movement to other parts of the country. He also organized several Library Conferences at various places to conscientize the States of the need of library activity. Iyyanki worked hard to further the cause of the Public Libraries among the peoples. He led "Library Pilgrimages" to the villages and made libraries to be the Centres of Rural Development. For Iyyanki, to start libraries in rural areas was a deeply-felt need.

Iyyanki has been the embodiment of Public Library Service. He even devised a scheme of Classification for village libraries. It was due to his untiring work and later that of Dr. S.R. Ranganathan, that the system of giving Government Aid to Public Libraries came into practice in 1920, which created a library consciousness in India. We can thus say that Iyyanki was instrumental in bringing about a national awakening of the library movement in the country from its early beginnings.

Besides establishing several Library Associations of Public Libraries at the state level in the following states:

Andhra Pradesh in 1914
West Bengal in 1925
Madras in 1928
Punjab in 1929,

he also established the All India Public Library association at the National level in 1919.

Mr. Iyyanki met his successor Dr. S.R. Ranganathan at Madras in 1927. It was at this period that marked the beginning of the Library Movement in India which led to the foundation of the Madras Library Association as well. Dr. Ranganathan, Speaking later of Mr. Iyyanki, remarked that Iyyanki was neither a Librarian nor was he a Learned man. One is not sure, says Ranganathan, whether he was even given to much reading. Yet, he was working tirelessly for the establishment of the Library Association in the various States of our country.

We find a similar coincidence in the two English speaking countries, namely, U.S.A. and in U.K. It was Andrew Cornegie who influenced the building of libraries in these two countries. In spite of his being economically poor, he worked tirelessly to bring about a Library Movement in the State. Later, this library education in the State and his involvement in libraries created a greater interest among the people for the existence of libraries. We also read that in the Western countries, many schools and colleges have been established by persons who had no benefits from institutions such as these. Sometimes revolutionizing discoveries and inventions have been often made by the non-educated and the unlearned persons. It we move in the world of science, we find that the steam Engine is the discovery of James Watt who was a mere clock-repairer.

This same history repeats itself in the 19th century in the formation of the Madras Library Association. It was Iyyanki who sowed the first seed of the library movement in India. Later, Ranganathan worked tirelessly to make this seed grow and flourish in several parts of the country. No work can be effective unless it is done systematically with a background and training. The library profession is not an exception to this. Library Training and Library Development of services go together.

Dr. Ranganathan, a professor of Mathematics and Science, was another Giant in the field of librarianship in India. After his graduation at the Presidency College at Madras, he became a Lecturer at the same college in 1917. While in his teaching career, he was persuaded by a friend to follow the library profession. Hence, Dr. Ranganathan left the teaching post as it did not bring him much income,. and proceeded to London for his training in Librarianship. He returned to India in 1925 as a full-trained Librarian. On the strength of this training and experience he gained abroad, he began working with great enthusiasm to start a library development through a proper functioning of the libraries in India.

Between 1924 and 1974, he developed new techniques, new ideas, new innovations and new methodologies. All this knowledge was based on his experience in the working of libraries abroad. Still remaining in contact with Iyyanki, his Guru and Leader, Ranganathan developed new tools for the working of the modern libraries in the country. By now Iyyanki was well advanced in years and felt happy that Ranganathan was dedicated in his work for the improvement of libraries.

Seeing that our Indian Libraries were developing in its own independent direction, Ranganathan got himself busy defining some unifying principles for their proper and systematic development in order to make them serviceable to the people. Thus in 1931, Ranganathan promulgated the "FIVE LAWS" of Library science. These are Service Oriented Laws which help the libraries even today to be the efficient Agencies of Social Change.

1. Books are for *use*
2. Every *Reader* his book
3. Every *book* its reader
4. Save the *time* of the reader
5. Library is a *growing organism*

Today, the development of libraries is based very much on the modern development of Science and Technology. In order to expand library and information services, there is need to use satellite communication system like, the video-techniques, and television programmes. To further the progress and development of library services, there is need of support through machine aids for the preparation of documents and other informational records.

Library development can be brought about more forcefully by enacting the Library Legislation. It is through Legislation that provision can be made for technical assistance to deal with library and informational activities. Inspite of the efforts of the modern library movement to make itself active for more than half a century, a clear picture of library profession and of the library functions has not yet been visualized in the country.

7

Changing Concepts of Public Libraries

Definition

The concept of Public Libraries dates to a few centuries only. In fact, there were no public libraries in the past. Libraries were attached to Educational Institutions in the Buddhists Monasteries, Mathas, Temples and Universities, like Takshasila, Nalanda, Amaravati, Vijayapuri and so on. In the middle ages Muslim Rulers and the Moghal Kings were the patrons of learning and of libraries.

Dr. S.R. Ranganathan defines the Public Libraries as :

- any library established or maintained by a local library authority, including the travelling and service libraries.
- any library open to the public free of charge and maintained and managed by the Government or by any local body.
- any library notified by the Government as Public Library.

A public library is distinguished from a private library or a subscription library. A private library is one which has a restricted ownership or membership. A private library is owned by an individual or by an institution or by an organisation. A private library, therefore, can be personal, institutional or it can be run by a voluntary organisation which is either registered or un-registered, as these usually collect fees for services. A free library service provided by a Charitable Trust is still regarded as a private library.

A library established by the Government and which collects fees is considered to be a Subscription Library, although it serves the public as a Public Library. In order to function as a true public library, it must have two characteristics - it must render free services to all and it must be established from the public funds. We cannot say that libraries serving the general public are public libraries. They could be either private or subscription libraries owned by voluntary organizations. Such libraries can also be classified as aided and non-aided libraries. Some such libraries charge a membership fee and take deposits for home-lending of books. These type of libraries extend their services to all its community members.

USESCO in its Public Library manifesto framed in 1949 and revised in 1972, states the concept of modern public library service as:

> "a practical demonstration of Democracy in Universal education as a continuing and life-long process in the appreciation of the achievement of humanity in knowledge and culture. It is a practical means whereby the records of man's thoughts and ideas and the expression of his creative immagination are made freely available to all. It is concerned with the refreshment of man's spirit with the provision of books for relaxation and pleasure and with the provision of up to date technical, scientific and sociological information."

The same Manifesto further defines the characteristics of a public library thus :

- "Started and maintained under the 'clear mandate of the Law'."
- "Maintained wholly from the public fund."
- "Free to all sections of the community, regardless of race, colour, age, sex, nationality, langauge, status of level of educational attainment."

The Advisory Committee appointed by the Government of India in 1958, advocated the internally accepted definition of a Public Library. It reads - 'It is a library which' :

- is financed for the most part out of public funds.

- charges no fees from readers and yet, it is open for full use by the public without distinction of caste, creed or sex.
- is introduced as an auxiliary Educational Institution providing means of self-education which is endless.
- houses learning materials giving reliable information freely and without partiality or prejudice on as wide a variety of subjects as will satisfy the interests or readers.

Finally, we have the definition given by UNESCO as well as by IFLA which reads :

> "that Public Libraries are those rendering services to people of a community or a region either free or with a nominal fee."

This definition removes all distinction between public libraries, private libraries and subscription libraries.

A Public Library is then, one which is open to all users and helps to satisify the threefold needs of the readers, namely, Educational, Informational and Recreational. Public Libraries of this kind are organized by the Government, by Societies, by Local Bodies, by Trusts and by Institutions. Public Libraries like other Educational Libraries can be established, managed and developed under a Legislature Act or by Administrative Rulers or by a private initiative.

The term "Public Library" brings together two concepts, namely; 'Public' and 'Library'. A simple definition of a public library would therefore be, that its existence is brought about by a town or by a country Council at its own expense. Such a library is governed and administered by the D.P.I. or by a Committee. As such, a public library offers a wide selection of reading material to satisfy the interests of every individual in the community or in the society. It is an institution whose aim is to foster self-education. It is the only effective Repository of our cultural heritage. A public library is often referred to as the "Mind of the Society". It is also called a "People's University", for it provides information to every citizen of the State and it has two important functions - namely, to entertain and to educate.

Functions

The functions of a public library are four fold and can be enumerated as follow:

(1) A public library as an Educational Centre has to promote and support all types of education - formal, non-formal, adult, and life-long education.

(2) A public library as a Cultural Centre has to promote culture. This can be done under two aspects, such as:

- *Reading* which is thought-provoking and which widens mental horizons and develops creativeness in an individual.
- It *contributes* to the cultural enrichment of the society. This is feasible by organizing extension activities like Seminars, delivering of lectures, symposia, book exhibitions and arranging for social and cultural gatherings or programmes.

(3) A public library has also to be an *Informational Centre*. It is not confined only to render information through reference service, but the services of a Public Library have to be extended to provide information on socio-economic needs of the society. A public library as an informational centre, is a specialized source of information. In rural areas a public library offers information regarding employment opportunities, public utility services and undertakes programmes of the Development Department. These form the essential areas of information which a Public Library is called upon to collect and to disseminate it to the general public in various forms of services to meet the needs of every individual in the society.

(4) The function of a public library is also to *provide* for recreational needs of the public. This is a very important function by which an individual is helped to spend the leisure hours in a healthy recreational way. Hence, the public library has to provide the reading material selected under periodicals, newspapers and light reading. Other recreational forms like Audio Visual materials, films, television, cassettes, records, also increase greatly the use of Public Libraries. Art, like painting/dancing, also help to make the public library a social recreational centre.

The Public Library being a part and parcel of the public, it has to keep contacts with the public for whom its existence is meant for. The term "Public Relations" (P.R.) is a most fitting term and which means "Communication".

Allen Angoff in his book *Public Relations for Libraries* defines P.R. as -

> "Public Relations in library and information centres is to communicate the essence of the library to the appropriate audience, to the public for whom it has so much to offer in order to fix the library in the mind as a source of priceless value."

The various types of users of the public library could be divided into the groups :

(1) The internal group which includes Administrative Officers and the Library Staff who need to be informed about the changes that take place in policies.
(2) The external group which includes Legislators, Civic Leaders and the general public.

Through its services to these two types of groups, the Public Library fosters community relations and a strong goodwill among the various sections of the community.

UNESCO states that the Role of Public Libraries is to offer both children and adults, opportunities to keep in touch with their times; to educate themselves continuously and to keep abreast of progress in Science, Arts and Technology. These functions require a constant reviewing, to be kept up to date and be attractively represented. This service would help the adults and children as well to form their own opinionss in life, to develop their critical capacities and powers of appreciation. The function of a Public Library is mainly concerned with communication and dissemination of ideas in whichever form they can be expressed.

A Public Library is intended to serve informational, educational and recreational needs of adults, children, the aged men and women, the blind, physically handicapped, mentally retarted, socially handicapped, the sick, prisoners, etc. In other words, a Public Library has to serve one and all the public without discrimination of caste, colour, creed and sex. For this it needs a sound Public Relations Programme (PRP) and which could be reached out through :

1. Use of Media
2. Special Programme
3. Personal Contacts
4. Atmospherics.

Although the well known media to reach out to the public are Audio, Audio Visual and Television, Pamphlets, Bulletins, it could also include ratio, posters, newspapers and periodicals, annual reports and souvenirs and lists of additions in the form of Book Lists.

The Public Library is a natural cultural Centre for the community and brings together people of similar interests. Cultural Programmes sponsored by the public library are events to help readers to know about the library, about the society and its culture and about what goes on in the world. These programmes can be of various types, such as :

Film Shows
Exhibitions
Talks and Lectures
Drama and Concerts
Debates and Discussions
Childrens' Programmes
Poetry Reading
Story Telling
Classical Music
Displays

A Public Library is also expected to render additional services to special groups within the community - To children through well-equipped childrens' section; to women in places where there is a strong social influence and women are put in the background. These women are considered as a special category; research scholars who belong to a highly intellectual group and need selected materials, the non-indigenous groups of people in community who require public services in their own languages. Besides, there are those physically and psychologically disabled persons who generally seem to be neglected as a group of the library. The sick and the prisoners come into this category.

A Public Library is also required to build contacts with the academic libraries, community organizations, adult education centres, business and industrial communities.

The location of the Public Library should also be central, attractive, and easily approachable.

Types

A library being a growing organism, it involves the organization of network of libraries on a hierarchal and territorial basis. Traditionally. Public Libraries are divided into Urban Public Libraries and Rural Libraries. The Urban public libraries form the State level public library system. According to this system, the Public Libraries are divided into :

- State Central Public Libraries
- Regional or Divisional Public Libraries
- District Public Libraries
- State City Central Public Libraries

In the Rural Public Library system, the public libraries are further divided into :

- Sub-Divisional Public Libraries
- Block Public Libraries
- Village Public Libraries and
- Municipal Public Libraries

In rural areas, the District Library is considered as the Central Public Library which is again divided into Block Public Libraries as it branches out.

In addition, there are also Government Aided and non-Government Aided Public Libraries both in the urban and rural areas. These are further divided into several categories. This division is based on the size and strength of its collections.

The State Central Public Library is able to serve a large population with a network of branch libraries. So also, a State City Central Public Library can serve a population of 50,000 and a State

City branch library can serve a population of 25,000 for a tutorial unit.

Management

The Management of Modern Libraries today has grown so complex in nature that it is no longer the rule of the thumb as it has been till about two and half decades ago. For the library management to be successful in modern libraries, it requires an intelligent scientific approach. In many of the larger and special libraries, the work of management is allotted to Library Specialists. To every library Manager, the managerial techniques pose a thought-provoking question namely

"Libraries : Are They Manageable"?

Though managing a library is almost similar to managing any other organization as far as the concepts, theories and principles of management are concerned, it is slightly different in the sense that libraries are essentially :

- Service Organizations
- Non-Profit Organizations
- A part of a larger Organization

In this context, we can say that a library management is concerned with general and simple terms like :

(1) Evaluation of activities and services for proper justification before authorities
(2) Effective response to the users' needs
(3) Meaningful use of manpower, finance, reading materials, equipment, so as to bring about improvement of library services
(4) Developing cost-effective work methods
(5) Developing staff and organization under various pressures.
(6) Developing attitude of staff to accept change.

When we compare these elements of management with the Public Library System in our country, we fall far short of its aim and purpose in practice. The Public Library System especially in North India and in the country as a whole lacks uniformity. This lack of uniformity is seen from the records of those public libraries in the States where Library Act is not yet enacted.

A proper management of libraries will get the staff involved in its works of management. A library can work or function effectively only when there is an effective management of the library staff. It is the staff efficiency that makes all the difference in our libraries.

If the Public Libraries have to meet the aspirations of the modern society today, serious thought has to be given to the various elements of staff management, such as, recruitment, selection of job analysis, number of staff required, and so on.

Finance

In order to organize any library, it is not enough to have a good staff, good administration or managerial skills. With all these our libraries will be just a theoretical dream. To function as living libraries, they need finance to support its work and its growth. And so, we find that finance is another important element of library management. Without adequate funds, no matter how perfect the library system and how efficient its services or its well-equipped staff be, it will not survive.

The Fundamental requirement of a really satisfactory service is to operate and to maintain the library services to an approved standard for which adequate funds is a necessity. The efficient services, the success, the smooth running and the expansion of any library is very much dependant upon the right use of funds at its disposal. Though the library is a non-profitable institution, funds available have to be used wisely and effectively.

The finance for Public Library Sevices is provided by the Government Funds or by Special Funds which are created by means of cess, donations, subscriptions, or by combined sources. This standard of distributing funds to Public Libraries is followed by the Raja Rammohun Roy Library Foundation in Classifying the Public Libraries of India for rendering financial assistance.

To render a free library service to all the sections of the public, a Public Library cannot be supported by public funds alone. It needs resources like;

- the local taxation
- Central and State Government grants
- Income generated from services to users

But the major share of the finance has to come from the State Government which is the responsible authority for the functioning of the Public Libraries in the State. The Public Libraries are also sometimes allowed to collect nominal charges from the users or for any special service rendered to them. As all these resources are limited, there is need of financial assistance from the Central Government as well.

The Recommendations from the Advisory Committee for Libraries drawn up in 1959, by the Ministry of Education, Government of India, states that:

- only a cess can provide a stable base for the library finance.
- this cess must be supplemented by grants from the Central and State Governments.

In the States of Maharashtra and West Bengal, the libraries do not collect cess but only a nominal fee from the users. The Karnataka Public Library Act has widened its base of surcharge to other taxes like, the vehicle tax. In Tamil Nadu and in Andhra Pradesh there is a surcharge over property tax. These amounts however, are too meagre to be able to make any impact on the finances of the Public Library.

Today, the Raja Rammohun Roy Library Foundation offers financial assistance to many States Public Libraries on the basis of a matching grant for the purchase of books depending on the requirements of the libraries.

For the voluntary organizations rendering Public Library Services, there is a scheme of assistance grant from the Department of Culture, Government of India. However, whatever funds are received from the Central Government, they are too meagre to cover up all the resource position of the State Public Libraries.

8

Public Library System in an Indian State

Today India has a Library system that services the population of more than 800 million (figure of 1988) in an area of 3.3 million square kilometres. The population is spread over in 2,643 towns and 5,75,000 villages.

Taking a look at the Public Libraries in India, we find that 15 States out of 22 (i.e. 65%) have Central Public Libraries, 291 Districts out of 400 (i.e. 73%) have District Central Public Libraries, 1,798 Development Blocks out of 5,027 (i.e. 36%) have village libraries, and 1,280 towns out of 2,645 have town libraries (i.e. 48%) out of 29 metropolitan cities of which 4 (14%) have city public library system with Central Public Libraries, Branch Public Libraries and Deposit Public Libraries. We find these Centres with Central, Branch and Deposit Public LIbraries in the cities of Madras, Bangalore, Hyderabad and Delhi.

In this chapter I would like to highlight the condition of the Public Library System in the State of Bihar. However, the condition prevalent in Bihar is repeated in many other States of our country. Hence, Bihar does not stand as a singled out State except for the author's survey of the Library System.

The Library Movement in India began in 1850, but it was only after 1948 that the movement became active. The library movement in India received its impetus from Dr. Annie Besant's Home Rule Movement. As a result the following major libraries were established in the State of Bihar:

The Khuda Baksh Oriental Public Library, at Patna, an Internationally known library was established in 1891.

The Bhagwan Pustakalaya Public Library at Bhagalpur, stands as one of the first library established in 1913.

The Smt. Radhika Sinha Institute and Sachchidananda Sinha Public Library at Patna, commonly known as the Sinha Public Library was established in 1922.

In spite of the deplorable and discouraging scene of Public Libraries in our country and in the State of Bihar, we can still hope for the best in some of the Public Libraries in the State, which today earn much appreciation. Institutions such as the Khuda Baksh Oriental Public Library is an outstanding institution for Higher Learning and Research. It is famous for its choicest and finest collections of Arabic and Persian Manuscripts and for its magnificent specimens of Persian calligraphy. It renders various kinds of services for dissemination of knowledge.

Besides the three major Public Libraries established earlier, there are today about 5,000 Public Libraries of various types in the whole of Bihar. It has not been possible for the author to survey all the existing Public Libraries in the State. The survey remained limited only to the Public Library System which existed in the Capital of Bihar, which is Patna and the following Public Libraries came under the survey:

(1) The Central Public Library (Sinha Public Library)
(2) The Gandhi Sangrahalaya Public Library
(3) The Government Urdu Public Library
(4) The Sadaquat Ashram Public Library
(5) The Gait Public Library and Institute
(6) The Prabhawati Mahila Pustakalaya
(7) The Bihar Hitaishi Public Library at Patna City
(8) The Gaya Public Library

The Public Library System in the State of Bihar includes both the village and the State level libraries. Until the beginning of the twentieth Century, libraries in India were confined to towns only. These town libraries functioned only to serve those readers who were educated. Apart from the vernacular libraries, there were also the Audio-Visual sections for the illiterates. The early statistics show that out of 706 libraries which were established in 1910, 661 libraries were started in the villages. However, the concept of rural libraries did not become popular in the country until independence. Libraries are social institutions of change and are therefore considered as effective instruments of social change in the modern society.

Information today is a national resource and a fundamental energy affecting all human activity. It is an indispensable power and it needs to be placed at the service of the whole community. It is only the Public Libraries that can provide access to documentation and information free of charge to all. A public library can help with information for the various sections of the community, such as, farmers, businessmen, children, housewives, and so on. A Public Library can create among its readers a love for reading, eventually cultivating reading habits. A public library can provide job information and help to pursue self-education. A public library can also serve the informational needs of the blind, invalids and prisoners to solve their social problems and create a political and social awareness among them. A public library thus becomes an Agent in the process of social change in the society.

Education forms the back-bone of a nation's progress and strengthens the fabric of a nation. It helps to produce persons of vision, integrity, character and intellectual citizens. All this cannot be achieved fully unless the library which is the component of the Educational System is strengthened to play its proper role. The air of the New Education Policy is to reach out to the distant illiterates and neo-illiterates. To emphasize the statement of non-formal system of education, the role of public libraries becomes very significant.

The survey of the Library System in Bihar showed that during the pre-independence period, the Government of Bihar had played an important role in the field of Education and the Library Movement. In the year 1935, after the Government of India Act, the Ministry of Bihar re-organized the methods and the functions of Education in the State. As a result, the First Bihar Library Association under the title of the Bihar Rajya Pustakalaya Sangh came into existence in the year 1936.

The need for network of rural libraries was realized as early as in the first decade of the twentieth century. In 1937 with the granting of the Provincial Autonomy to the British Provinces, the political leaders and the social workers did take an active part in the mass literacy movement. In the State of Bihar, Dr. Syed Mahmud, the then Education Minister, started the movement with much success. The

Advisory Committee for libraries set up in 1957 under the Chairmanship of Sri K.P. Sinha, suggested measures for the improvement of the libraries. This marked the milestone in the history of the Library Movement in the State of Bihar.

In 1972, the Raja Rammohun Roy Library Foundation came into existence for the promotion and development of the rural libraries. The Five Year Plan of 1973-78 organized the rural library services in the district of Karnataka. The rural library scheme is of recent origin and it needs a serious effort to strengthen the Public libraries to play their role in the implementation of the National Programme.

The tradition of Learning in Bihar has been strong since ancient times. Libraries have always been considered necessary and vital for learning. The University of Nalanda was a renowned seat of Learning with a well-equipped Library. The Gupta Dynasty had assigned the revenue of many villages for the maintenance of Nalanda.

Unfortunately, with its destruction, the tradition of Public Libraries can be said to have dissapeared. The Buddhist Monastary of Pataliputra, also had a very big library attached to the institution. So also, we find that during the medieval period, there existed Temple Libraries in Bihar. These libraries were considered as seats of Learning at the time.

If we enter into the details of the existence of libraries in the State of Bihar, we learn that there existed huge libraries on the Banks of the River Ganges. These libraries were situated at Azimabad at Patna City. They contained large collections of Persian and Arabic literatures. The remains of these mighty buildings can still be seen today by any interested traveller. Besides, the private collections and manuscripts of poets and nobilities also formed good libraries of rare collections. These libraries were found at Mujubia Khanqush of Phulwarishariff, at the Imadia of Patna City, at Khalifabagh of Bhagalpur and at Ishlampur. The treasures of Urdu, Persian and Sanskrit books and manuscripts are now scattered in various villages and towns of the State.

The libraries of modern Bihar have also played an important part in the field of Education and Library Movement. Realizing the importance of libraries in a Democratic State like Bihar and to eradicate the problem of illiteracy, the Government of Bihar has made efforts to establish, to develop and to strengthen the Public Libraries at different levels. Most of the Public Libraries in Bihar are

Government-aided and are located in the urban as well as in the rural areas. The growth of libraries at various levels in the State has provided opportunities for a life-long self-education to the reading community. The public libraries in the State, no doubt, do meet the needs of the general public covering the various aspects of life.

During the pre-independence period, the influence of libraries was greatly felt in the State. But today, a closer look into the functions of these libraries presents a poor picture due to lack of cooperation from the State Government and its meagre financial aid for the development of the Public Libraries. The earlier libraries were set up as part of the Community Development Projects which were begun in 1951. Each of these projects for social Education had a budgetary provision under which old libraries could be supported or new libraries set up. These libraries remained as small units only. Since independence, many Government-Aided libraries have been set up to promote social education.

Today the Public Library System and the Library Movement in Bihar is given a forward push by the Founding of a New Library Association which bears the name BILSA. This Association newly founded in 1987 aims to promote the Library Movement which has been at an unorganisational standstill since 1964. The First Library Association, which has already been mentioned earlier, had started its work in 1936. But its organisation having been fallen into the hands of non-librarians over the years up to 1964, it remained inactive. And, as such, it could not work for the progress of the Library Movement in the State.

The main work of the new association is to strengthen the position of libraries and that of the librarians at all levels in the State. It also works to enthuse the Government Officials to realize the need for granting Library Legislation for the State. BILSA today works with the energy of the "Youth Wing" at its forefront. Its activities are further strengthened by receiving grants from the Raja Rammohun Roy Library Foundation since 1988.

All the efforts of BILSA even with the Youth Wing working tirelessly for the uplift of the Library System in the State of Bihar seems to be of no avail. Unfortunately, the Government of Bihar having no funds to maintain not only the libraries in the State but is also unable even to provide proper and adequate funds to run the Educational Institutions. As a result, the works of the Association are at present at a standstill.

9

A Case Study

The case study of Public Libraries in Bihar could be divided into four sections:

Section A : The Structure of the Public Libraries
Section B : The Management of Public Libraries
Section C : The Finance of the Public Libraries
Section D : The Staffing Pattern of Public Libraries.

The case study refers to a personal survey made by the authoress and the study of the Reports of the Public Libraries of 1984 as well as that of 1989. There have been no recent reports available for the years after 1989. The Report of the Public Libraries under the control of the Superintendent of Libraries, Bihar, Patna, had the following public libraries on records:

(a) The State Central Public Library at Patna
(b) The Divisional Central Public Libraries
(c) The District Central Public Libraries
(d) The District Sub-Divisional Public Libraries
(e) The Divisional Public Libraries
(f) The Special Public Libraries.

SECTION A

The Structure of Public Libraries

The Public Library System in Bihar consists of one State Central Public Library at Patna. This library is commonly known as the Sinha Public Library.

The Divisional Central Public Libraries are established at Muzaffarpur, Dumkha, Bhagalpur, Ranchi, Hazaribagh, Saharsa and Gaya. The District Central Public Libraries are set up in 25 districts (excluding the District Headquarters of Madhubani, Sitamarhi and Samastipur). Out of these, 22 public libraries are Government-aided and the rest are run by private management. Except for a few District Central public libraries and the District public libraries, the condition of all other District Central public libraries in the State is quite deplorable due to improper allocation of funds from the State Government.

Under the First Five Year Plan of the Bihar Government i.e. between the year 1953-54, the public libraries were established in seventeen districts of the State, namely, in Patna, Arrah, Gaya, Bhagalpur, Monger, Santhal Parganas, Champaran, Darbhanga, Chapra, Muzaffarpur, Ranchi, Hazaribagh, Dhanbad, Purnea, Palamau, Chaibasa and Daltongunj. Out of these, the public libraries in twelve districts, namely, Patna, Arrah, Gaya, Bhagalpur, Monger, Champaran, Darbhanga, Muzaffarpur, Chapra, Hazaribagh, Palamau and Daltongunj, were converted into District Central Public Libraries. These twelve public libraries are administered by the private managing committees. In five districts i.e. Ranchi, Dhanbad, Purnea, Santhal Parganas and Chaibasa, the Public Libraries were converted into District State Public Libraries. These five libraries are fully financed by the State Government and are controlled and administered by the Education Department, Government of Bihar, Patna.

Today, Bihar has 39 District Public Libraries. During the past few years, nine sub-divisional Public Libraries have been raised to the status of District Central Public Libraries. These public libraries are controlled by the District Education Officer. At the District level, the Public Libraries are poorly administered. The District Sub-Divisional public libraries are located at Vikram, Barh and at Nalanda.

In 1956 Mobile Library Service was introduced in these districts. The Scheme provided one Librarian, one Driver and one Mechanic. The scheme was drawn up with an aim so as to reach out to the readers who were far from the district public libraries. The Project, however, received an yearly grant of Rs. 7,680 from the State Government. This amount was granted per unit so as to meet the expenditure of the staff salary, fuel and other contingent items. But the amount being inadequate, the efforts to work out the mobile library scheme were a failure. It could not continue beyond 1975. Together with this scheme, there was also introduced scheme for children's libraries. Part-time staff was appointed by the State Government for these services. Having to face the same problem of inadequate funds, the scheme has to be closed down the same year.

The Divisional Public Libraries are established in ten districts headquarters. These are known as Commissionary Level Public Libraries and are located at Darbhanga, Bhagalpur, Muzaffarpur, Chapra, Saharsa, Gaya, Ranchi, Hazaribagh, Patna and Dumkha. Out of the total 86 sub-divisions in the State, there are only 29 sub-divisional public libraries. In many of the new sub-divisions, no public libraries are yet established.

Out of 588 blocks, only 440 blocks have public libraries. There are about 67,566 villages in the State of Bihar. But the Directory of Public Libraries shows the existence of 4,422 village public libraries. The Report of 1989 records less than 4,000 village public libraries in existence.

The special public libraries are six in number. They are :

– the Gait Public Library, Gardanibgh, Patna
– the G.N. Public Library, Bharatpur, Patna
– the Prabhawati Mahila Charkha Samiti, Kadamkuan, Patna
– the Sharda Sadan Public Library, Lalganj, Vaishali
– Sri Hindi Pustakalaya, Sheoarai, Nalanda
– Sri Gyan Niketan Pustakalaya, Parsauni Chowk, Sitamarhi.

A further survey of the Public Libraries in the State, brought to light that the existence of public libraries was graded under two categories, namely;

A – the classsified public libraries, and
B – the unclassified public libraries

The source of this finding was the Education Department, Government of Bihar, Patna.

There are 61 Classified public libraries in the State which fall under Category A. These can be summarised thus:

(i) State Central Public Library (Sinha Library), Patna	1
(ii) Divisional Public Libraries (after up-grading)	10
(iii) District Central Public Libraries	25
(iv) Sub-Divisional Public Libraries	19
(v) Special Public Libraries	6
Total Classified Libraries:	61

The State Central Public Libraries in Bihar are of two types:

(i) the fully Government-aided Public Libraries
(ii) the non-Government-aided Public Libraries

The fully Government-aided public libraries are six in number. These are located in the districts of Ranchi, Dhanbad, Purnea, Chaibasa, Bhagalpur and Patna.

The unclassified public libraries falling under Category B are also of two types:

(a) Block Public Libraries	440
(b) Village Public Libraries as per records	4,000

The unclassified public libraries are controlled by the S.D.O.

The Village Public Libraries are further classified into four divisions. This division is based mainly on the following factors:

– library collections
– land acquisition
– size of the library building.

The grant for these libraries is also divided accordingly. Thus we have the four divisions of Village Public Libraries in the State receiving the following grants :

Category A : Rs.100 to Rs.150
Category B : Rs.100 only
Category C : Rs.40 to Rs.70 only
Category D : Rs.30 to Rs.40 only.

These amounts do not make any provision for the payment of the library building rent nor for the salary of the staff, not even to the part-time Librarian. These two factors are completely ignored by the Government. These factors also create a problem for the management of these libraries.

The Director of Higher Education, Government of Bihar, Patna, assisted by the Director and the Superintendent of libraries, is responsible for all the Public Libraries in Bihar at various levels. At the District level, the S.D.O. who is also the Secretary, is responsible for the working of the Public Libraries in the various Districts.

There is however, much development to be made for the progress of the village libraries in the State. According to the suggestion made by the Planning Commission, one village library is to serve a population of 1,000. But the actual records of the State show that for population of 15,000 there exists at present only one village public library. Besides, the existing village libraries lack proper equipment, reading materials, and reading facilities. Moreover, there is not even a qualified Librarian to organize and to manage these libraries. All these handicaps come in the way of creating a proper public library development in the State of Bihar. In such a situation and with such poor efforts towards the growth of public libraries, the existing libraries fail to be effective Centres of Education at the Village level. Most of the village libraries in Bihar are established through voluntary organisations.

Comparing the study of Village, Town and District Public Libraries of Bihar with those of five other States where Library Legislation is implemented; we have the following figures in Table 9.1.

The statistical figures show that much improvement has yet to take place in order to bring about a successful Library System in the State of Bihar. This improvement as well as the progress of the Library System depends very much on the enactment of Library Legislation. There is however hope that the efforts and struggles of BILSA to bring about an awakeing of this development of Library Movement in Bihar in the near future, will be a success if the Government becomes favourable to acknowledge the worth of libraries in the State.

TABLE 9.1 : Statewise Libraries

States	Yr. of Start	No. of Village Pub. Libraries	No. of Town Public Libraries	No. of District Central Pub. Libraries
Andhra Pradesh	(1960)	1,623	207	21
Karnataka	(1965)	1,698	230	19
Maharashtra	(1967)	285	257	29
Tamil Nadu	(1948)	3,427	–	18
West Bengal	(1979)	531	61	16
Bihar	(1989)	4,000	39	1

SECTION B

Management of Public Libraries

Management of libraries is an important function, and is concerned not only with its resources but with the staff management and the other functions of the library. It is the efficient power of the management that makes the libraries effective Centres of Education and of social change. This requires the use of several management techniques. These techniques can be applied to all the functions of library services and works. Often, the use of computers especially today in modern libraries can help to solve many problems of the management in libraries.

Management involves a lot of planning especially where Public Libraries are concerned. Public Libraries being institutions of social change, are institutions of learning. Hence, extension services is one of its important functions. There is a vital need for the public libraries today to conduct user surveys, seminars and organize lectures for the people. The essential role of a good public library can be realized only by trained librarians.

By nature, a public library is a continuing and a growing organization. Services to the public must be backed by modern medias and above all with financial resources and sufficient staff to make the dervices effective to the users.

The above concept of Library Management is but a theoretical one. Most of our public libraries in the country fall far short of this ideal. Comparing the practicality of these few concepts with the public libraries in the State of Bihar, we find that the libraries in the State are completely neglected by the Government authorities. The existing libraries have neither the proper and sufficient qualified staff nor do they have adequate funds to be able to manage its works and to make them the essential institutions of learning in the State. Many of the Public Libraries are ill-managed for lack of trained Librarians being appointed to manage and to organize them.

The details as to how these libraries work in the Capital of Bihar is given below. This information has been collected personally by the authoress.

The Smt. Radhika Sinha Institute and Sachchidananda Sinha Library, Patna

This library popularly known as the Sinha Public Library, owes its existence to the great generosity of the Late Dr. Sachchidananda Sinha, Bar-at-Law, who founded both the Institute and the Library in memory of his wife, Smt. Radhika Devi. It was her desire that the rich collections of this Institute should be made available to the general readers. The collections of this library are more that 85,000 Volumes.

Originally this library was founded by the State Government in 1924 and it was known as the State Public Library of Bihar. At this time the library had been one of the most influential Government Public Libraries. Later, the library was gifted to the State of Bihar by Dr. Sachchidananda Sinha, the first great Journalist of Bihar. Dr. Sinha as Reader, as Journalist and as Bibliographer was fortunate in having a big collection of volumes as books were available at a very low price in those days. All of Dr. Sinha's leisure time was spent in reading, thus cultivating a great love for books which later developed into the form of a library. Today this library stands as a big monument not only of a happy conjugal relationship, but also with a sense of genuine goodwill and service for the community of its readers.

It is a large and spacious two-storey building. It has in its holdings valuable cultural treasures, which have made a great contribution to the cause of Education in Bihar. Today this mighty building is not spacious enough to hold the growing number of collections and the increasing number of its readers.

Besides the general collections, there is quite a big collection of Rare reading materials such as:

History of India in 8 Volumes (1859-77)
Martial Races of India - 1900
Cambridge History of India in 2 volumes: 1921-28
French Revolution in 3 volumes
Collection of Oriental Works in 7 volumes: 1874-79
Leaders of Public Opinion in Ireland in 2 volumes: 1911-12
History of Ireland in 5 volumes : 1913-17
History of Britain - 1912
Affairs of East India Company in 2 2 volumes : 1917-18
Fifth Report of East India Co. Affairs - 1812
History of English Education in India : 1781-1893
Gazetteers : Mysore
Imperial Government of India in 35 voumes
District of Bengal, Bihar and Orissa in 36 volumes

District of Great United Province in 35 volumes Various Congress Reports in 80 volumes from 1892 onwards National Congress Proceedings from 1895 onwards

Moral material and condition of India in 100 Volumes from 1882 onwards Indian Home Rule, 1917.

The library was given the status of the Central Public Library through an agreement made between the Trustees of the Institute and the Government of Bihar in 1955. Today this library stands as a noble monument having valuable treasures. It renders effective services to teachers, students, scholars and the enlightened public of the State.

The library is well used for study as well as for research work not only by the students of the various countries in India, but also from countries like Germany, Australia, Canada, U.K. and U.S.A. Besides the large collections of books, the library has in its holdings a rich collection of journals, periodicals and of newspapers (old and current) and which are not available in the neighbouring libraries of the State. All this reading material is greatly used both for study and for research purposes. At present the library has in its holdings about 1,50,000 volumes. The library works effectively with a minimum staff strength of 30 to 37 employees only which includes professionals and peons.

Besides these facilities, the library has also created various other sections, such as, the reading room section, local literature section, children's section, the Braille section and the Research section. There is a future plan for the construction of another additional block depending on the Govternment-aid, to extend the library facilities to the public.

Other Public Libraries

A further detailed study of other existing Public Libraries in the Capital brought to light that very few of them are making real progress but even this progress is restricted with several problems. For example,

The Gandhi Sangralaya Public Library

This is the only library in the State which is being developed with a rich collection of literature on all the great revolutions of the world. It is one of those libraries which is most in keeping with the modern trends.

The Government Urdu Public Library

This library is one of its kind in the State and in the country. It is directly under the control of the State Government. It is a very popular library. For the past fifty years, this library has played a very important role in the social, cultural and educational life of its community.

The Sadaquat Ashram Public Library

This Ashram Public Library grew up at the start with great aspirations of our First President of India, Dr. Rajendra Prasad. But today it has not been able to make any progress due to the lack of Government-aid.

The Bihar Hitaishi Library of Patna City

This library was founded in 1883. It is the second oldest Public Library in the State of Bihar. During the pre-independence days, it was an important Centre of social and political activities. It did play a very significant role in promoting socio-cultural values in the life of its community. Today this very institution is getting almost insignificant to the public due to lack of cooperation of the State Government.

The Prabhawati Mahila Pustakalaya

This is the only women's library in the State of Bihar. It still functions with two untrained hands. The library is at present languishing for want of funds for equipment, book collections and the staff.

The Gait Public Library

It is a small Government-aided two-room library. It is a library which defeats its purpose of existence. It is a library far from what it should really be and it hardly deserves the name of a Public Library today.

In the neighbourhood of the State Capital, we have two other Public Libraries at Gaya District.

The Gaya Public Library: This library was founded in the year 1855 and is the oldest modern public library in the State of Bihar. It is managed poorly and it faces many problems which do not enable it to function in an efficient manner.

The Mannu Lall Public Library of Gaya : This library possesses a very rich collection of Sanskrit and Hindi books. It is rarely visited by scholars who would be enriched with the use of its rich collections.

The Management of Public Libraries in the State of Bihar is very much dis-organised and deplorable. The only way to make the Public Libraries in the State as well as in other parts of the country to render effective and efficient services, is through the enactment of the Library Act. At present only six States in India enjoy the Library Legislation and the Public Libraries in these States are flourishing. The States without the Library Act are still waiting for the final decision of their State Governments.

Although the Extension Services form a part of the Public Library Services, no public library in the State of Bihar is yet engaged in such works. In fact, the Bihar State Government has no future plans in this direction. However, in the event of Public Libraries planning to take up Extension Programmes, such as, Adult Education, Book Exhibitions, Creating Readership Awareness, and so on, they are to be seen to by the Trust of each library with the consent of the Central Public Library through the Education Department.

The D.P.I. is responsible for all the Public Libraries at all levels in the State of Bihar. The Deputy Director is also the Superintendent of Public Libraries and Inspector of the State Public Libraries in the State. At the District level, the S.D.O. is also the Secretary and Inspector of the District Public Libraries in the State.

SECTION C

Finance of the Public Libraries

A Public Library is one that is financed out of public funds, and readers use its collections free of charge irrespective of caste, creed or sex. But in reality this is far from the real and practical functioning of the public libraries. The Government grants allotted annually are never sufficient to run the libraries in an efficient manner. The amount available for equipment or for book purchase in order to make the libraries grow and flourish is inadequate. The financial crisis are so accute today that even the monthly salaries of the staff are not being paid regularly to those employed in library services. This chapter gives a detailed picture of how the finances are allotted to the State Central Public library in Bihar for its own use and for the use of other public libraries in the State.

The State Central Public Library is financed by the State Government. During the years 1970-92 the total expenses incurred by this library are shown in Table 9.2.

TABLE 9.2. Yearly Total Expenditure

Year	Total Amount Rs.
1970–1974	8,86,000.00
1979	1,71,187.00
1980–1981	3,30,000.00
1981–82	5,98,000.00
1982–83	3,75,431.00
1983–1984	3,32,585.00
1984–85	3,80,585.00
1990	33,00,000.00
1991–92	45,66,368.00

Source: Education Department and Central Public Library.

These amounts cover up the expenses on Non-Plan and Plan Heads of Expenditure as well as expenses incurred on the Library building.

However, Table 9.3 gives a detailed expenditure of the State Central Library under various heads of expenditure for the years 1970-92.

TABLE 9.3. Detailed Expenditure of the Central Public Library

Year	Establishment	Non-Plan Bks., Furn., periodicals	Plan Period Furn. & periodicals	Building Fund
	Rs.	Rs.	Rs.	Rs.
1970–74		–	–	8,86,000.00
1979	1,71,187.00	–	–	–
1980–81	2,37,305.65	–	–	–
1981–82	2,95,000.00	64,694.35	28,000.00	–
1982–83	3,20,431.00	55,000.00	48,000.00	2,00,000.00
1983–84	3,08,278.00	55,000.00	–	–
1984–85	3,02,310.00	24,307.00	–	–
1985–86	–	30,275.00	48,000.00	–
1990	–	27,00,000.00	3,00,000.00	3,00,000.00
1991–92	7,66,368.00	29,00,000.00	6,00,000.00	3,00,000.00
Total	24,00,879.65	58,29,276.35	10,24,000.00	16,86,000.00

Note : There has [illegible]n no grant for establishment during the years 1970-74; 1985-86; and 1990.

The budgeted amount to run the various public libraries in the State during the years 1980-85 under the Plan and Non Plan Heads are given in (Table 9.4). A total amount of Rs. 24,22,400 for the Non-Plan Head and Rs. 7,80,500 for Plan Head was granted to the Central Public Library and this continues to date. Both these amounts are inadequate to meet the expenses of all the public libraries at present at various levels. However, no figures have been available in the Education Department, Government of Bihar, Patna for the years 1970-79 and after 1985.

TABLE 9.4. Annual Budget for Public Libraries for Plan and Non-Plan Heads: 1980–1985

Year	Div. Libs.	Dist. libs.	State Dist. Libs.	Special libs.	Block libs	Non-Plan	Plan
1	2	3	4	5	6	7	8
						Rs.	Rs.
1980-81	2	23	24	6	440	5,16,000	–
1981-82	2	24	25	6	435	6,66,300	–
	–	28	16	7	32	–	5,11,500
1982-83	2	24	25	6	431	6,64,500	–
1983-84	2	14	–	5	–	5,75,600	–
1984-85	–	15	9	7	–	–	2,69,000
	–	5	17	–	–	–	–
				TOTAL	Rs.	24,22,400	7,80,500

The Government of Bihar had spent a total sum of Rs. 30,17,332 on the various public libraries during the Fifth Five Year Plan of 1978-84. Besides this amount allotted by the Government, the Raja Rammohun Roy Library Foundation made available another small sum of Rs. 16,200 only to the State Central Library. This amount was used to purchase books which were later distributed to the select public libraries in the State as shown in (Table 9.5).

It was further learnt that the National Policy for Libraries and Information Systems had set aside 6 to 7 per cent of the total Budget for the purpose of Education during the year 1988-89. But nothing has been made available so far for the working of these two systems. The annual expenditure on Education in Bihar is about Rs. 350 crores, while the annual budget for public libraries in Plan and Non-Plan is Rs. 3,00,000.

The Government-aided libraries receive an annual grant to meet the expenses on construction work, building repairs and for purchase of furniture as in (Table 9.6). The figures of the budget sanction have not changed since 1980-83 to suit the modern context of rising prices. No figures were available for 1970-79 and after 1983 when the author surveyed the financed department in 1989.

TABLE 9.5. Records the Expenditure on various Public Libraries in the State of Bihar 1978–84

Year	Amount of Expenditure	State Central Lib.	Dist. Central Lib. Dist. libs. Sp. libs	Sub. Div. libs.	Block Libs	Village libs.	Total Libs.
	Rs.						
1978-79	4,29,487.75	1	31-7	25	110	200	364
1979-80	4,08,999.25	1	31-7	25	210	310	564
1980-81	6,04,984.60	1	31.7	25	113	310	487
1981-82	4,34,879.50	1	31-7	25	175	310	549
1982-83	6,60,317.50	1	31-7	25	175	310	549
1983-84	4,78,653.50	1	31-7	25	100	394	559
Total	30,17,332.10				Total Libraries		2,513

Source: Govt. of Bihar, Patna.

The Public Libraries as such do not receive any funds for equipment nor for the repairs of the library building. The funds are sanctioned for the purpose of book purchase, appliances and for the payment of Establishment only.

TABLE 9.6. Budget sanction for Government-aided Public Libraries during 1980-1983

Year	Building construction Rs.	Building repairs Rs.	Furniture Rs.
1980–1981	2,09,900.00	—	24,000.00
1981–1982	2,41,900.00	21,000.00	20,500.00
1982–1983	—	21,000.00	20,500.00
Total	4,51,800.00	42,000.00	65,000.00

Source: Education Deptt., Govt. of Bihar, Patna.
There has been no change for 1992 in the figures.

Further the pattern of current existing expenditure is seen in Table 9.7. There is no allottment of funds for the payment of Municipal Taxes and the Telephone Bills of the Public Libraries. The Village Libraries suffer likewise.

TABLE 9.7. Governemnt Grants for the various Public Libraries during 1989 onwards

Public Libraries	Grants for Books	Grants for appliances	Grants for Establishment
	Rs.	Rs.	Rs.
State Central Public Library	3 lakhs	(cover all the items)	
District Central Public Library	6,000	2,000	Paid according to the number of staff employed
Sub-Divisional Public Libraries	3,000	1,000	
Divisional Public Libraries	8,000	4,000	
Special Public Libraries	5,000	1,500	

Source: Education Department, Bihar.

The employees of the Public Libraries are paid a minimum Basic Salary and this too is not being paid regularly. The records show a sanction of Rs. 16,000 only per annum per library for the payment of the employees working in the District Public Libraries. The Sub-Divisional libraries receive an amount of Rs. 10,200 only for the same purpose. There is however, a promise from the Education Commissioner to raise the amount for the salaries of employees in various Public Libraries in the State during the next budget session 1992. But due to the crisis in finances, the Education Deptt. has not been able to keep to its promises.

During the First Five Year Plan, the State Planning Committee had proposed to supply television sets and a Photocopier to the State Central Public Library as well as to all the District Public Libraries. For the success of this scheme, there was an agreement with the State Government for a matching share of two to five lakh rupees per year. This new and promising feature of development has yet to materialize in the near future when the problem of financial crisis is solved in Bihar.

The Government-aided or Classified Public Libraries as they are called, receive a total grant of Rs. 3 lakhs for the purchase of books, for equipment and for establishment. The District Central Public Libraries receive an annual grant of Rs. 6,000 only for the purchase of books. They also receive another additional grant of Rs. 2,000 only for the purchase of appliances. The Sub-Divisional District Public Libraries get an annual grant of Rs. 3,000 only for the purchase of books and an additional grant of Rs. 1,000 for the purchase of appliances. The Divisional Public Libraries likewise are allotted a grant of Rs. 8,000 for the purchase of books and another additional grant of Rs. 4,000 for appliances. The Special Public Libraries receive a sum of Rs. 5,000 to be spent on books and another sum of Rs. 1,500 to be spent on appliances (Table 9.6).

The Unclassified or non-Government-aided libraries, receive only an Assistance Grant. This grant is too meagre for the survival of these libraries as seen in Table 9.8.

TABLE 9.8. Annual Assistance grant to Non-Aided Govt. Public Libraries

Type of Libraries		Amounts
Divisional Libraries	Rs.	82,140.00
District Libraries	Rs.	61,600.00
Sub-Divisional Libraries	Rs.	32,120.00
Special Public Libraries	Rs.	3,000.00

Source: Govt. of Bihar, Patna.

The public libraries set up before 1972 received a grant of Rs. 3,000 only. Unfortunately, the inadequate allocation continues to date in the case of these libraries.

Looking into the finances for the Block Public Libraries, the statistics reveal the existence of 588 Block Divisions in the State. But, only 435 Blocks have libraries establilshed and these libraries receive an adequate grant of Rs. 300 only per annum per library.

Except for a few District Central Public Libraries and the District Public Libraries, the official statistics bring to light that the annual sanction of funds for the public library system are far from being adequate. The Village Libraries are, however, financed by the Superintendent of Libraries. This is the wing of the State Education Department, Government of Bihar.

There is a clear illustration in Table 9.9 to prove that the current spending on Public Library System in the State of Bihar is awefully inadequate. This is the main explanation of their languishing condition. Hence, there is a vital need to increase inputs in this direction if our modern library system is to give effective services to the users.

TABLE 9.9 Funding of the Public Libraries in the State of Bihar

Libraries	Annual grant Central/ State Govts.	Trust Fund	Grants from Supdts. of libs.	Other Grants	Remark
1	2	3	4	5	6
	Rs.	Rs.	Rs.	Rs.	
State Central Public Library Patna	1,83,000/- varies from two to four lakhs	50,000/-	–	2,000/-	fully financed by the State Govt.
Prabhawati Mahila Charkha Samiti Public Library, Patna	10,500/- for books & appliances	–	100/-	–	salaries to librarians from 'Angan Wadi Scheme'
Gait Public Library, Patna	5,000/-	–		–	
Khuda Baksh Oriental Urdu Library, Patna	1,00,000/- (Central Govt.) 15,000/- (State Govt.)		–	–	receives Plan Grant of Rs. 25 lakhs, (Central Govt.)
State Urdu Public Library, Patna	17,000/- to 1,00,000/-		(for books and appliances)		

Source : Each of the Library Records survey report.

Comparing the Public Library network in India, U.K. and U.S.A. through the statistics of 1970-72 (Table 9.10), we find that the total expenditure for education per annum in India is more than in U.K. and in U.S.A. and that of U.S.A. is much more when compared with U.K. The inadequacy of funds to meet the expenses of the Public Library System in India, causes a dis-organised functioning of the system in the country.

TABLE 9.10. Puble Library Network in India, U.K. and USA.

Item	India	U.K.	U.S.A.
Total Expenditure on Education per annum	Rs. 11,000 million (1971-72)	Rs. 8,789 million (1970-71)	Rs. 3,83,370 million (1970)
An Expenditure on Public Library per annum	Rs. 30 million (1971-72)	Rs. 6,000 million (1970-71)	Rs. 12,480 million (1970)

SECTION D

The Staffing Pattern in Public Libraries

Staffing becomes an important function for organizing a Library System. This demands much planning and it requires a strong managing power. There has to be a sound employment forecast so that right ppeople are placed at right jobs at the right time, and in the right place. This can only be carried out by an organized structure.

Before a staff is appointed, one has to be acquainted with the important characteristics of a well-designed library system, such as, its effectiveness, efficiency, dependability, flexibility, simplicity, and acceptability.

The staffing pattern in various systems will differ. This difference will depend on the factors such as,

(1) objective of the Institution
(2) its organizational structure
(3) quality of library services it renders
(4) type and number of users and the depth of services rendered.
(5) time duration of services
(6) building facilities and service conditions

In a library with computer system, the staffing pattern will be quite different from that without the computer service.

A look at the Andhra Pradesh Public Library Staff Structure given below, brings to light that the structure has been implemented by certain norms.

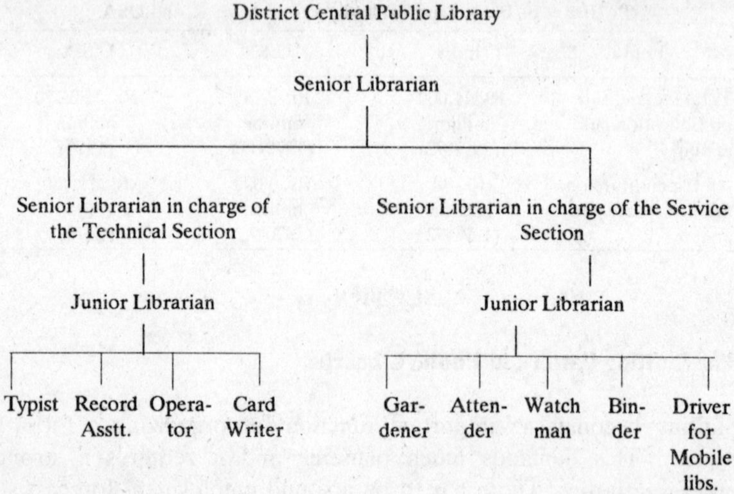

The above staffing pattern suggested by the Workshop in the District Library System of A.P. is on the pattern that could be adopted in all the Public libraries of A.P. Hence, the library organizational Committee has made a thorough study of the problem of staff pattern in public libraries.

As seen from the structure, the District Central Library has three senior Librarians. One is in direct control of the Management while the other two are mainly concerned with the functional structure. This staff pattern has now been categorized for the Branch Libraries which are based on the services rendered. Accordingly the Public Libraries are classified into four grades based on the minimum volume stock and library service (Table 9.11)

Table 9.11 Grades of Public Libraries

Grade		Total Volumes in Stock	Annual lending of volumes
Grade A	:	20,000 books	25,000 books
Grade B	:	8,000 books	12,000 books
Grade C	:	5,000 books	7,500 books
Grade D	:	less than 5,000 books	less than 7,500 books

Having no uniform pattern of staffing, the committee of Andhra Pradesh Public Libraries, has recommended certain norms for the appointment of the staff over the State of Andhra Pradesh. The grades for the appointment of the Librarians are again divided into four divisions as seen in (Table 9.12)

Fig. 9.12 : Division of Public Library Grades

Division of grades	Grade I Librarian	Grade II Librarian	Grade III Librarian	Grade IV			
				Record clerk or Attender	Gradener	Watch man	Binder or Helper
Grade A :	1	2	3	2	2	1	2
Grade B :	–	1	–	1	1	–	–
Grade C :	–	–	1	1	–	–	–
Grade D :	–	–	1	–	–	–	–

The Recommendations further state that, for the Central Public Library which is not in Grade A, will still have the provision of:

one gardener
one record clerk or attender
one watchman
two binders or helpers.

For the Public Libraries, the staff will be appointed according to the norms recommended by the committee.

The staffing pattern in the State of Madras is again different from that of other States. The staffing pattern for the Madras District Central Public Library is divided into two sections:

A-Librarians
B-Ministerial staff

Again, these two sections are further divided as follows:

Section : Librarians

Grade I	3
GradeII	6
GradeIII	8
Record Clerk	3
Garderners	4
Watchmen	2
Binders	2
Helpers	2

Section B: Ministerial Staff (Differs in various districts of Madras)

Local Library Authority	Supdt.	Asstts.	Jr. Asstts.	Typist	Record clerk or Attender	Grad-eners
Madras :	1	3	3	3	2	3
Districts other : than Madras						
Dhamapuri :	1	1	2	1	1	2
Dharmapur :	–	–	1	1	1	2

If we compare the staffing patterns of Andhra Pradesh and that of Madras with Bihar, we find that it is again different. The staffing pattern for the Government Public Libraries in the State of Bihar is fixed by the Education Department, Government of Bihar, and is as follows:

DIRECTOR

DEPUTY DIRECTOR

Section Officer | Asstt. Section Officer | Finance Officer | Special Secretary in financial matters of the Education Deptt.

The sanctioned posts in Government Public Libraries other than the State Public Libraries is as follows:

LIBRARIAN

Assistant Librarian

Sorter | Binder | Peons | Night guard | Gardeners

The qualifications recommended for the library staff working at the State Central Public Library are as follows:

Librarian	:	B.A., Lib. Tr. (one/six months to 2 yrs.)
Asstt. Librarian	:	Matric, Lib. Tr. (one month)
Sorter	:	Matric Certificate
Binder	:	Binding Certificate

Obviously, the Public Library is top heavy and appointments are hardly ever seen to at the functioning levels, thus retarding the services to the public.

Comparing these three staffing patterns of three different States, namely, Andhra Pradesh, Madras and Bihar, the picture that presents itself is, that there is no uniformity whatsoever. In order to maintain uniformity of staffing patterns and staff appointments, there should be certain standards drawn up by the Central Government or by a Committee appointed for this work.

Standards will not only help for proper staff appointments and to have a systematic staffing pattern, but standards will help in the proper organization of the functions of the libraries. Standards will enable the library authorities to place proper persons at proper jobs, at the proper time and in the proper places. Only then can we expect to have a uniformity of staffing pattern and of staff appointments which will lead in the unitormity of library functions.

10

Adult Education

Realising the importance of adult education programme today and to meet the challenges of illiteracy in our country, there is need to emphasize the importance of A.E.P. through the Public Library System.

Since the promotion of adult education is a function of the Public Library System, it would be fruitful at this stage to trace the background of Adult Education in the State of Bihar. The records of the Adult Education Departmant, Government of Bihar, show that the Education Department does not take any responsibility for the adult education through the public libraries. The Adult Education Department is independent in its work. The Government of Bihar inaugrated this programme for Adult Education in the State in the year 1978. But, it started its work only in the month of April 1979. A year later, this project was taken up more seriously and a village programme was conducted in 31 Blocks in 31 Districts of the State. One person was made responsible at each Block to carry out this programme.

A project Officer was appointed to supervise over the working at each Block. A stock of books was made available for selected work groups at the village level. According to this system, the books were lent to the village workers and to the neo-literates. They were guided in the use of this material and the material was collected after its use. The Officer-in-Charge was paid a minimum stipend of Rs.100 only per month for every group of 150 learners. But the local village workers did not show any interest in this project. The result was that the system failed to function successfully in the fulfilment of its plan.

Later, in 1983-84, a different strategy was planned by the Adult Education Department. This plan involved a ten-month programme for Adult Education. The programme demanded that the learners be divided in the age groups of 15 to 35. Each Block was then divided into five Learning Centres with a group of 30 learners at each centre. A total of 150 learners at each Block was supervised by an Officer-in-Charge.

The learners were divided accordingly after testing their mental abilities into three categories of groups A, B and C. These three groups were further divided into groups of A1, A2, A3, and so on. The self-learning materials were graded into three independent sets in literature and in arithmetic. The learners received guidance in the use of reading materials. Exercises for study were given under instructions. Each group of 30 learners at each centre was given homework for six days. Villagers were free to choose their free time for study. The programme was carried on for 25 weeks i.e. for six months. At the end of this period, there was an evaluation of the study work. This strategy has been accepted by the village people and so it is being continued to date.

The idea behind this strategy is that through self-learning, the adults and the neo-literates would be able to start their own small village libraries to encourage reading and writing among the neighbouring villages. The strategy differs from Block to Block depending on the mental ability of the learners. It also differs from centre to centre in its pattern to suit the ability of the learners.

From my personal sharing in the experience of some of the village workers in adult education, it was very interesting to find that many of them could memorize beautiful poems and sayings from *Ramayana* and other religious scriptures. But they were not able to put them in writing as they had no knowledge of the alphabet. This creates all the more a vital need for A.E.P. especially in villages. The learners themselves have expressed in the course of their sharing, that by learning the alphabet, they would have the joy to see that what is in their memory is being put into writing. This felt need makes all the more necessary for a tie-up between Adult Education Programme and the Rural Public Library System.

The stress laid on A.E.P. underscores the importance of literacy. The literacy rate in India is about 35 per cent and it is lower in rural areas. This always poses a question as to how the neo-literates can be prevented from lapsing into illiteracy, the only remedy would be to set up network of village libraries. The Librarian is required in the network system to occupy the key position in the process of communication. Hence, a village Librarian needs to display posters dealing with socio-economic programmes in regional languages, organize exhibitions on current literature such as, agriculture, small scale industries, poultry farm, dairy farm and so on, to keep the village people in the know of the latest developments in these various fields.

This service also presents a need to discuss with the village people, the current problems pertaining to their interest, generate reading habits and keep in touch with the problems of the local people. Today the present condition of the rural library system in Bihar is deplorable. They are anything but effective operative Centres of mass communication. It has been stated by the National Council of Applied Economics at Delhi, that, "where property stands between people and books, it is the libraires that must act as a link between the books and the people". Could we make this a living reality in our village library system?

The eradication of adult illiteracy and the development of programmes for continuing education has been the major thrust of the Seventh Five Year Plan. This programme could be a success only when linked with the activities of the Extension Progarmmes of the Public Libraries. In order to hold these programmes, the Central Public Library has to have recourse to the services of the society. It is the responsibility of the State Government to meet this end, to establish and to develop the public libraries at the urban and at the rural levels. Each being the major responsibility, it calls for efficient steps to be taken to implement the public library development programme.

The Library Development in Adult Education in the Soviet countries could be a good example for India to start working on this programme on proper lines. The history of the development of Adult Education in Russia tells us, that before the Revolution the villages of Russia were educationally and culturally backward. The Revolution necessitated the re-building of the country by having recourse to national economy in order to eliminate illiteracy. This itself was a tremendous as well as an important task.

The village libraries were established in the Soviet countries, by starting reading rooms which formed the Centres of Education for the village people. In these reading rooms cultural programmes, book exhibitions and book displays were organized. The reading of newspapers in the reading rooms became an important activity for village people. Through this kind of reading the people became aware of the new innovations for various types of works.

The reading material like the magazines and newspapers were also distributed in the market places free of charge to create a taste for reading among the adults. Tea clubs were also opened to be the centres of attraction for discussion on topics of interests. These tea clubs were the focal points of Education and of Culture.

Further, to have a better knowledge of the needs and interests of the village people, books were read to them and their opinions were collected for evaluation.

The starting of children's clubs in villages was another incentive to make the love for books grow among the adults of the society. This attempt gave rise to the slogan that "in order to help the development of libraries in A.E.P., one has to be a friend of libraries". Krupskaya, wife of Lenin and a distinguished authority on Public Education in U.S.S.R., has said:

> "We cannot limit ourselves to simply passing degrees. The liquidation of illiteracy should be coupled with a library building campaign. We have much work ahead of us."

This is true when applied to adult education.

After the victory of Socialist Revolution, the Soviet State tackled the immense problem of illiteracy which plagued the young Republic. The leaders of the State realized that illiteracy was the greatest impediment to the development of the State. It took a vow to wipe out illiteracy within 20 years. Unlike other countries, they did succeed in achieving it. Network of libraries were established from village to National Libraries. Reading rooms in villages and clubs in workers' settlements was given a great importance. There was a great tie between the libraries and everyday life. Librarians worked with anthusiasm to popularize books. Through all these efforts a great change and a great progress was achieved in the field of Education including the A.E.P.

From 1920-40 as the Soviet History of Libraries has it, sixty million people were taught to read and to write. The progress in A.E.P., resulted in an ever-increasing thirst for knowledge among the adults. This in turn necessitated the growth of libraries and production of books in a rapid and planned manner.

All this was possible because the Soviet State created a State Fund for literature to restore the network of popular libraries which had suffered an extensive loss during the Nazi War (1941-45). With the help of these funds, the libraries increased by 12 per cent in the year 1950. Within a decade of 1953-63, U.S.S.R. was able to establish 32,000 State village libraries with increase of book collections to a large extent, which is seen in the following statistics:

TABLE 10.1 An increase in the number of libraries and their stocks at the beginning of the year - USSR

	1914	1935	1941	1965
Libraries (in thousands)	75	116	277	867
Stock of Books and periodicals (in millions)	46	299	527	2,331

On the eve of the First World War there ware 76,000 libraries of all types in Russia. During the year 1965 we find the total increase of libraries was five times more.

Further, the Census Report of 1934 reveals that 92,000 out of 104,000 registered mobile libraries belonged to the Public Library System. The public libraries amounted to 44 per cent in the Soviet State and 34,000 qualified Librarians out of 55,000 were employed in these public libraries. The statistics of the First Five Year Plan (1927-32) in Russia gives a detailed account of Public Libraries that existed in rural as well as in urban areas (Table 10.2). During this period there was a gradual increase in the number of libraries in the State.

During the pre-war years there has been a great development of network of public libraries in U.S.S.R. which is clear from the statistics shown in Table 10.3.

By 1986, the total libraries of all types in the Soviet State numbered 3,26,000 with more than 560 millions of volumes in its holdings. The total number of users using these libraries numbered to 234 million.

TABLE 10.2 Existance of Public Libraries in Rural and Urban areas

Year	In towns & Rural Areas		in towns		In rural areas	
	No. of Libs.	Stock (in 1000)	Libs.	Stock (in 1000)	Libs.	Stock (in 1000)
1927 :	26,492	69,202	7,538	43,521	18,954	15,681
1928 :	28,864	72,166	7,970	46,763	20,894	25,403
1929 :	29,249	79,636	8,964	54,113	20,985	25,518
1930 :	27,454	91,206	7,807	64,179	19,675	27,027
1931 :	27,737	90,399	8,546	59,582	19,191	30,958
1932 :	32,918	91,284	9,066	60,326	23,852	30,956

TABLE 10.3 : Development of Network of Public Libraries during pre-war years

Year	In towns & Rural Areas		in towns		In rural areas	
	No. of Libs.	Stock (in 1000)	Libs.	Stock (in 1000)	Libs.	Stock (in 1000)
1937 :	69,975	126,640	13,801	56,174	56,174	43,201
1938 :	77,775	147,573	15,952	98,377	61,823	49,196
1939 :	86,312	166,764	16,970	110,096	69,342	56,698
1940 :	95,401	184,767	18,454	120,593	76,947	64,174

Compared with the Soviet State and many other Western countries, India still stands among the most backward countries where education is concerned. Education in India has not yet made its way to the rural villages in a significant way. The majority of the population still remains illiterate and fails to enter into the process of change.

The need for network of rural libraries was felt as early as in the first decade of the twentieth century. Compared with the Soviet Union Library Movement, we can say that our country is much larger and it has a very fertile land. We can boast of a rich cultural and religious heritage. We have greater facilities for literature learning. With all this rich heritage, we , in India have not yet been able to reach out to our people with books. It is not that we are lacking in reading material. We have plenty of it. What is needed is a "Free Access to Books". The Free Book Service in Soviet countries has given rise to mobile libraries which today are very effective among the people.

There is a great need especially today of sharing of information between libraries, educational institutions and other Information Agencies. This would facilitate their informational needs and services through proper provision of postal and tele-communication rates. A deeper awareness of Library and Information Services could be given through instruction in the use of our public libraries and its informational resources, so that freedom to read is exercised by everyone and thereby encourage a free-flow information to all.

Libraries take their importance from the fact that individuals are not able to purchase books due to their exorbitent rising prices. It is the libraries that can help with the use of such books and reading materials to those who cannot afford to have access to them.

A poor administration and organization of our public library system records poverty of library services to its readers. Sometimes, even the librarians seem to be afraid of involving themselves to take risks to better th library services for fear of experiencing either reward or punishment for the good they would desire to do.

For effective Extension Services of a Public Library, there is need to draw up proper standards in which A.E.P. could also have a place. Having adequate resources without any fixed standards for services would be meaningless. Hence, mini standards especially for libraries in rural areas are prescribed. However, certain basic guidelines are necesary for any standards of Public Library Service. These guidelines could be comprised of:

(1) a primary unit library which should have three sections, such as;
Lending section, Reference and Reading facilities within the library.
(2) There should be an open access system to facilitate browsing through the material on the shelves even for adults in A.E.P.
(3) Though a charge of a nomianl fee is permitted for home-lending, no fee is to be charged for reading in the library or for using the library.
(4) There is need for Trained and Qualified Staff for organising information services, extension services, for circulation and for conducting the mobile library system for the handicapped and for special groups of readers and also in A.E.P. services.

(5) A proper cataloguing and classification system should be observed in Public Libraries, so that the library operations take on an effective preactical turn with all the readers.

(6) The Public Library Services must be linked with the District and State Public Library Systems, to ensure wider reading materials to the readers.

(7) The Public Library Services must have a regular evaluation of its house work, extension services and adult education programmes, by maintaining the necessary statistics.

The Raja Rammohun Roy Library Foundation is considering these guidelines and has undertaken the responsibility to draw up a Project for the preparation of a Public Library Service Standards for India.

As things stand today, the State Governments are responsible in each State for the promotion of Public Library Services in the country. Out of twenty-two States and nine Union Territories, only six States have adopted Library Legislation. i.e. Andhra Pradesh, Karnataka, Maharashtra, Tamil Nadu, West Bengal and recently the State of Manipur. The other States are working for it, while some other States are developing Library Services through administrative measures.

In North India, the major States are opting for grants-in-aid System for Extension of library facilites in small towns and villages. At the national level, we have the Raja Rammohun Roy Library Foundation as the Central Promotional Agency. A National Library Information Policy is expected to be adopted soon by the Indian Government. Larger funds for Library and Information Services have been planned in the Seventh Five Year Plan under the State and Central Plan sectors which has still to be implemented.

IFLA has been continuously reviewing the various standards. In a Democratic country like India, there is no other option but to experiment with various models of library development in different parts of the country.

11

Library Legislation

Efforts to implement the Public Library Act in the State of Bihar is a necessity. In 1935 after the promulgation of India Act, the Ministry of Bihar re-organized the methods and functions of Education. In 1938, the Bihar Association of Libraries presented a Draft to the State Government for the development of libraries in the State. This involved a network of libraries throughout the State and was approved by the Ministry of Education. Later, four thousand village libraries were established under the Mass Literacy Campaign.

The need for Library Legislation has been felt from as early as in 1940. Since then, several attempts have been made towards its enactment. Several attempts have also been made to submit Memoranda through the years 1973; 1975; 1978; 1979 and again in 1988 and in 1989 by BILSA. But nothing seems to have been done in this line to help improve the Library System in the State.

In 1973, the Central Public Library (Sinha Public Library, Patna), submitted a Draft Bill to the State Government. This Draft was drawn up by the then duly constituted Sub-Committee of some eminent Librarians of the time in the State of Bihar, such as Professor P.N. Gour, Dr. A.R. Bedar, Dr. R.S.P. Singh and some others in the profession. But sad to say, that Bihar is still struggling with various obstacles. The Bill seems to be resting on the shelves and the State Government is slow to take any action in this regard.

For a proper organisation of the Public Library System in the State of Bihar and to be able to remove illiteracy to some extent at least, there is need of effective library services to the public. The

Public Libraries as they stand today with deficit funds and lack of resources, cannot work effectively under the State Government unless Library Legislation is brought into force.

According to UNESCO guidelines, 'the Public Libraries should be established under the clear mandate of law so framed as to ensure nation-wide provision of library service'. On the basis of this guideline, IFLA has issued the following guidelines to help the Public Library System :

(1) There should be a Mandatory Legislation.
(2) A Central Authority should be charged with supervising the implementation of the Act.
(3) The Library Act should state the units with responsibility for providing Public Services. The Act has also to ensure financial arrangement for the Extension Services. This point was emphasized at the Seminar organised by UNESCO at Delhi, in the year 1955.

It was Dr. S.R. Ranganathan who first introduced the First Library Bill in our country and which resulted in a 'Free Library Service'. The Library Bill was first introduced in the State of Madras through the influence of his own student who then came into power. At Hyderabad the Bill was introduced as an outcome of a Seminar at which the Chief Minister of the State was invited to inaugurate the function. This paved the way for granting the Library Legislation at Hyderabad. At Mysore, the Education Minister happened to be the member of the Library Association with Dr. Ranganathan as its President. In the capacity of his power, the Education Minister was able to convince the Government Authorities of the need for Library Legislation in the State.

A similar event took place at West Bengal too. When the government of West Bengal came into power in the year 1979, one of its first efforts was to work for the library development. As a consequence, the Library Act came into force speedily. If we read the history of the Library Movement in Great Britain, we find that India got its Library Legislation through an M.P. Today in our own day we have the State of Manipur, since 1988, enjoying the full benefits of the enactment of the Library Act.

If all these States could so work for the Library Legislation through various ways, what can hinder the State of Bihar as well as the other States in the country, from working for it? Democracy gives us "Freedom" for action. It gives freedom for the development of individual talents, for starting various Associations for definite purpose, and what not. So too Democracy today can give us, librarians, the same freedom to work tirelessly for the enactment of Library Legislation that could make our libraries really effective as service institutions in the cause of Education.

Every library, whether academic or public, is an Universal Agency for Universal Perpetual Education. Hence our motto should be :

We want libraries for one and all
We want network libraries for one and all.

F.M. Gardner, conducting a study of Library Legislation, which was sponsored by UNESCO in 1971, made certain observations on some of the problems relating to Library Legislation. He opined that :

(1) it was for the State Government to decide whether the Central Authority for Libraries be independent or whether it should be linked to or be subordinate to a Government.
(2) that Public Library Service at the local level should be independent of other Agencies for its work.
(3) as regards finance and administration of Public Libraries, the State Government should see to its ideal development and its establishment in urban and rural areas.
(4) Legislation should also make provision to fit within the system the private or subscription public libraries. Attention should also be given for making provision towards cooperation and inter-loan services.
(5) each library should have the power to draw up the rules and standards for its functions.

Gardner finally stated that the Legislation is an instrument of authority and that no public library system or for that matter of fact, even the academic library system can exist without Legal Authority.

Although Legislation has been considered to be the best basis for the organisation of library services, we find that not only in India but also in countries like France, Belgium, the Netherlands and Itlay, libraries suffer for want of the enactment of Library Legislation.

Very few States in the developing countries have adopted Library Legislation. Without library ligislation, there can be no proper library system. In order that library system be what it ought to be, there is a vital need to devise some strategy in a country like India to organize the Public Library Services.

Referring to India, Gardner has observed that while the State Legislation may vary in its details, the Government of India should lay down three basic requirements, namely :

(a) Promotion of funds which is to be derived from three sources –

The Central Government,
The State Governemtn, and
Administrative Areas.

(b) Executive Powers should be given to the Department of the Central Government to make provision for progressive implementation.

(c) There must be clear direction which could be gradually observed into the Public Sector of Libraries.

The Central Government can pass an Act if the subject of 'libraries' is transferred from the State List to the Central List. The Government of India can set up institutions like, the U.G.C. by an Act of Parliament to promote library services through financial incentives and especialized guidance.

In fact, the Raja Rammohun Roy Library Foundation was established for this purpose in 1972. Besides, the preliminary giant work of Mr. Iyyanki, paved the way towards "Library Legislation" in the country. It was at this time that Dr. S.R. Ranganathan, the successor of Mr. Iyyanki and Father of Library Movement in India, who took the first bold step to introduce the First Model Library Bill in 1931. The State of West Bengal was the first State to want this enactment of the Bill. Attempts were made to introduce this Bill in its Legislature.

The Government at the National, and State level has the reponsibility to maintain and to establish a nation-wide Public Library System under the law. The growth of Public Libraries and Rural Development are very much dependent on one another. The rural development is indispensable of library services for the economic, social, cultural and Educational development as well in our contry. In view of the rapid development of mass media communication today, a co-ordinated system of information is being built up to change the attitude and behaviur of the Indian masses for bringing socio-economic change in the society especially in the rural society, as rural information is not possible without a constant flow of communication to the rural masses.

The progress of a community depends on the Information Processing System through which information is effectively transmitted to all potential users without any discrimination. Library is one of the effective means for this purpose in providing access to a wide range of written as well as non-book materials, such as, records, tapes, films and micro-films and so on.

The United Nations through its especialized agencies, particularly, UNESCO has already stressed the need of improved communication in support of rural development. If our country has to be prosperous, we have to make provisions of Free-Flow of Information to the rural masses to exercise their judgement. Rural libraries are effective means for raising the general cultural level of the rural people, moulding its general outlook and perfect operational skills.

The rural libraries can also act as an essential organization of all types of cultural and of recreational activities for the rural masses. Rural libraries can be organized as a focal point of mass Education. Rural libraries can also play a very important role in improving the economic condition of the community by providing commerical and technical information.

Finally, through the enactment of Library Legislation we could look forward to :

- A library system in each of the remaining States in the country.
- A network of libraries for the whole country.
- Regular finances to support the libraries.
- State responsibility to maintain and to develop all types of libraries.
- Free Access to literature.
- Free Book Service to All.

For a meaningful growth of Public Libraries there should be :

(1) The implementation of Library Legislation in each of the States for proper development of Public Library Services.
(2) Suitable machinery at the National level as well as at the State level be constituted for the purpose of co-ordinating the programmes of formal and non-formal Education and that of the library departments. For this purpose, a National Institute of Library Service should be opened.
(3) There should be a short and a long term Public Library Development for all Districts, Sub-Divisions and Block-Libraries in villages.
(4) Special care should be taken by the State Government for the preservation of rare books and manuscripts.
(5) Book grants for libraries should be increased in proportion to rise in prices of books.
(6) Reprographic and micro-graphic services be provided in libraries at least up to the District level in the first phase to improve quality in library services.
(7) One full-time paid staff in each Block and village aided libraries be appointed.

A Public Library as a social organization is also an instrument of social change. A Public Library is expected to play a part in promoting Distance Education by serving the needs of those undergoing such programmes.

The Library Profession is a Service-oriented Profession. It possesses the art of rendering services in a spirit of dedication in order to help humanity. Although the existence of libraries can be traced to ancient time, their role and function has changed today to suit the social, economic and Educational needs of the society. It is sad to note that India which was under the British Rule for 185 years and when she got her independence on August 15, 1947, there was not a single Public Library in the country. The British did not find it necessary to make use of the Library Law for India which was already passed in Britain since 1850. The State of New Delhi was designed in 1910 and completed in 1930. But no one felt the need at this time of having a Public Library in the State.

12

Resource Sharing

The resources of libraries are becoming inadequate day by day due to growth in literature and the rising prices of books and journals. Besides, the libraries have to face the shrinking budgets from year to year. The demands for information from the users too has increased tremendously in libraries. It is impossible for any modern library to work on the lines of being self-sufficient. In a country like India, where resources of most of the libraries are inadequate and unbalanced, it is extremely important to pool the resources of various libraries together for cooperative collection, organization and services.

With an expension of knowledge, a lot of literature is published and it is impossible for any library to cater to all the needs of its users. In the early twentieth century, this problem was solved by the first Library Cooperation started in England. It was felt that the collections of individual libraries should be exploited for the use of a greater number of readers. Hence, the Library Association and other Organisations in England recommends schemes to bring the libraries closer for instituting cooperation among them.

Resource sharing in academic libraries is even more important due to inadequate finances and personnel. Several Commissions like the Radhakrishnan Commission of 1948 and the Kothari Commission of 1964, had recommended that 6.25 per cent to 10 per cent of the Education Budget be allotted for expenditure on libraries. But it is disappointing to note that only 1.5 per cent is spent so far on most of the libraries.

Concept and Scope of Resource Sharing

Any organisation which is self-sufficient and has sufficient resources to carry on its activities, can be an example of the concept of self-sufficiency. Practically this is impossible. We need the cooperation of other libraries, because library work includes a number of activities. No library can afford to possess all the materials to meet the various needs of the users. In library cooperation, we cannot pin-point any specific area where we would need cooperation. Resource sharing includes any and all library activities such as, collections, functions and services. Resources also include personnel, funds and all that goes to fulfil the aim and objectives of any library. Resource sharing is therefore, a substitution for Library Cooperation. Today Library Cooperation is still on the idea plane. Some libraries however, are devising ways and means to make efforts towards library cooperation.

In order to enter into this scheme we need :

- To modify and change our internal library system.
- To feel the need for collaboration.
- To bring about a whole-hearted agreement for collaboration
- To work at having standardization, uniformity and consistency in our efforts for collaboration.

What is Resource Sharing

Resource Sharing is that which one can turn to as help in time of need. In other words it means to contribute something which one owns to benefit others. Resource sharing can apply to various commodities, where libraries are concerned. Resource Sharing can be applied to the sharing of collections, funds and personnel. Today every library whether large or small, faces the lack of these elements in some form or the other. This problem is faced not only by the libraries in India but also by those in the Western World. Resource Sharing implies partnership. It is the sharing of library functions in common by a number of libraries in the specific area, locality or region.

Pre-requisites for Resource Sharing

To start a Resource Sharing System certain requisites are required, such as :

(1) Accessibility to the holdings of any library by each participating library which should be clearly spelt out.
(2) Standardization of library techniques.
(3) Building up of specialised collections in each of the participating libraries so as to bring about the sharing of these collections with other libraries.
(4) Specification of loan period.
(5) Implications of finances.
(6) Provision for compilation of Union Catalogue.

Resource Sharing enables the sharing of library resources with a wider category of users, instead of libraries remaining as isolated units without any channel of communication. The area where Resource Sharing can be possible would be :

- Inter Library Loan
- Union Catalogue
- Cooperative Acquisition
- Cooperative Cataloguing

The Inter Library Loan services certainly increase the use of library resources through co-operation and coordination among the individual libraries. It consists of lending and borrowing of books, providing photo copies of articles, permitting users of one library to use other libraries and so on.

Union Catalogue of books and Serials form an important tool for knowing the availability of resources in the cooperating libraries. Union Catalogue is also an essential tool for facilitating the use of Inter Library Informatin.

Cooperative Acquisition of Library materials, serials and other documents which are not easily available can be undertaken by the participating libraries. This will include the acquisition of rare publications brought out by the Foreign Agencies and which cannot be purchased nor thought of acquiring by any individual library.

Cooperating Cataloguing is another area of activity which can lead to economy by avoiding unnecessary duplication of efforts although this is a difficult task at the start.

The Need and Purpose of Resource Sharing

The need for resource sharing techniques comes from the rapid growth of information centres and literature, the capacity for storage, financial constraints and rise in the cost of publications. Every year we have more than three lakhs of new titles published in Science and Technology and more than seventy thousand periodicals. We can add about a thousand more to each every year. The yearly output of publications can be estimated to be about fifteen to sixteen million documents. It is humanly impossible for any library to acquire all these publications and it is much more impossible for readers to have access to them. The only way to meet this situation is to have recourse to resource sharing.

The Third and the Fifth Law of Library Science promulgates :

> "Every Book its Reader", and
> "Library is a Growing Organism".

In the light of these two laws, no library acquisition can meet all the demands of its users, except through resource sharing device. The two important factors that make resource sharing a possibility are :

- Reading materials that cover the library works of Classification, Acquisition, Cataloguing, Storage and Preservation of documents.
- Resource sharing relates to library services in the form of Inter Library Loan and Book Exchange.

The purpose of resource sharing is to bring about the following results :

(a) An improved library service to users giving them a greater accesss to library materials and services like the CAS, SDI, and so on.
(b) That every potential user of the library meets his or her needs without loss of time.

(c) The provision of better services at a less cost than when undertaken by any induvidual library.

(d) Development of information, which is a new term and which today is becoming a dominating factor in decision-making and research work. This information is utilized not only for decision-making and research work but also for problem solving. Information technology relates not to collecting of this information, but also for processing, using and marketing purpose.

Success of Resource Sharing

The success of resource sharing depends on the following components :

(a) *Cooperative Acquisition* : The reading materials acquired by certain libraries are very much in demand by the users. By cooperative acquisition, wasteful expenditure and duplication of reading materials and storage problems would be avoided. The costly foreign periodicals which otherwise is impossible to purchase would be purchased within this system.

(b) *Book Exchange* : All the duplicate copies of books and of periodicals from various libraries in a particular area of locality would be collected in a central place under the Central Organization. These materials than would be exchanged with other libraries. This sort of exchange system can help to avoid books and periodicals from being in a dead stock. The system also assures the maximum use of reading materials.

(c) *Cooperative Storage* : Resource Sharing also involves the establishment of Depository Library at the local and regional levels, by a group of cooperative libraries. The less-used reading materials of cooperative libraries is stacked together here by a compact storage method, and are broadly classified. The access to this material is through Bibliographical Tools.

(d) *Technical Processing* : The resources of various libraries are pooled together at a Central Place for classification and for cataloguing. When this work is centralized at the National or at the Central Library, the processing is done by the Unit Card System. These Unit Cards are then purchased at a nominal cost by the various cooperative libraries. This avoids duplication of processing work and there is saving of time and personnel.

(e) *Cooperative Binding* : This work involves agreement between the various libraries under cooperation to bind books and periodicals at a Central Place. No single library can afford to have a binding section and to provide for its maintenance. The Cooperative Binding System can employ the modern equipment and binding can be done at a cheaper rate and in lesser time.

(f) *Cooperative Training* : In many of the College/University/Public and Departmental libraries, the staff lacks experience and professional knowledge. This knowlege and experience could be gained and enriched by the sharing of personnel and by exchange of library services on temporary basis within the locality or within the region. Experts from other cooperating libraries could also be loaned to help in this training of work experience.

Sometimes, staff from other libraries could also be deputed to work in libraries where there is lack of staff so that the services to users in these libraries do not suffer. Where University and Departmental libraries are concerned, a library system could be organized with the Central Library as a Co-ordinating Agency.

(g) *Cooperative Library Service* : These services become necessary due to the tremendous growth in reseach activities, increase in output of information and the increase of users' demands. The collection of books, storage and dissemination of such a big amount of information is beyond the capacity of any individual library, however large a library may be. To enter into this sort of Cooperative Library Services, it requires that there be data-bases in the form of catalogued information in a given time, in a given library and in a given discipline. This information could then be computerized for the benefit of other libraries. The data-bases can be accessed by a mutual exchange with various Agencies in the locality, through membership of network producing data-bases. So also cooperative S.D.I.

and C.A.S. Services can be had by the distribution of subject fields to be covered up by the libraries of a particular locality.

The situation of information explosion can be tackled only through Centres having Sectoral Information Centres and Local Information Units as planned and worked out by NISSAT. NISSAT network comprises broadly of :

Sectoral Information System
Regional Information System and
Other Specialized Services

NISSAT is the contact-point to provide quick and efficient services for the whole country.

(h) *Inter Loan Library Services* : REYNOLDS defines this System thus :

"It is a technique by which one library lends its materials to any individual reader through another library."

In other words, through this system, a library broadens its lending services to include materials which are made available by other libraries for meeting various needs of users in the surest, quickest and economical way.

The Inter Loan Services supplement the resources of a library and creates a confidence in the library users that a needed document can be had wherever it may be available. In countries like, U.K. and U.S.A. these services are well advanced. In India, such services need much support and encouragement from the Government authorities and it likewise needs a willing cooperation on the part of the libraries and the library authorities. In some parts of our country, this service is in its infancy stage still. The main questions that pose problems for the progress of Inter Loan Services are :

(1) who will benefit from its services?
(2) what material is available in which library?
(3) what material could be listed in this service?
(4) what policy should be framed for its organization?

The Inter-Loan Library Services can operate at various levels – local, regional, State, Naional and also at the International level. Its success depends on a well-planned library system for promotion of Inter Library Loan Service. The National Central Library should serve as the International Loan Centre for the country and be the APEX of this System. The Reprographic Services should be extended by the National and the State Central Libraries who should also maintain the Union Catalogue.

The effectiveness of the system can be had only with the enactment of Library Legislation Act. The Act should make the Provision clauses on resource sharing giving importance for its need and effectiveness. It should also provide for finances and the way for conducting the library services.

Besides Library Legislation, the Resource Sharing Scheme can be a success depending on the following factors :

(a) A willingness on the part of the cooperating libraries to enter into this system
(b) To have sufficient reprographic services.
(c) Efficiency of communication and postal services.
(d) Adequate Bibliographical Centre giving information of the available resources in the participating libraries.
(e) Sharing of the owned materials by various libraries
(f) Agreement on acquisition policies
(g) Agreement on Bibliographical and Standardization procedures.
(h) Defining period of loan, renewal and replacement of lost materials.

Resource sharing can teach us to manage the libraries in a more effective way and bring about a joint working of library services. It would also benefit the library users to a very great extent.

In the face of the problems facing the modern libraries, resource sharing seems to be the only solution. The use of computers, the modern networking system, Union Catalogue and Cooperative Library Service provide effective resource sharing facilities. However, it must work on a right plan, framing the right policy for action or else, resource sharing remains an empty service without the achievement of its goal.

The major factors that effect networking of libraries are :

- availability of communication facilities
- standardization of library organizational practice
- availability of financial resources
- efficiency in the governance of networks.

Resource sharing among the libraries having literature on common field of specialization is a must today as no library, however large, can afford to meet the enormous needs of all its potential users. It cannot afford to collect, store and disseminate all the available information on any topic individually. For a successful implementation of resource sharing activities, there is need of creation of Data-bases by means of automation or Computer services at various levels. This in turn, may be combined into bigger Data-bases known as Data Banks in cases of long comprehensive listing of all materials available in participating libraries. Their proper and up to date maintenance can easily be done with the use of computers.

The development of a nation depends on the access to information as pointed out by a Nobel Laureate in Economics. The modern libraries must now be inter-dependent for procuring of information. The developing nations need to develop such a network for sharing the information on the basis of Resource Sharing so that duplication of books is avoided, thereby helping the libraries in drawing their budgets on book buying. This will enable researchers to get more information for their research activities as well.

13

User Education

The new outlook of the Educational System multiplies its impact on libraries very much. Due to changes in the societal structures and teaching methods, students and teachers rely greatly on library services. The growth in the research-oriented studies and expansion of knowledge in every field, have added to the importance of academic libraries. The lack of staff and other facilities in college libraries, do not permit to meet the challenging needs of the users today. Some of the college libraries are not even able to provide the basic needs for its users. Today, much stress has been laid on the technical aspects of the library and the needs of the users tend to be over-looked.

Changes are taking place in the outlook of libraries in the way the users are facing the emerging information age. The old concepts and tradition of library use are undergoing a tremendous change due to the Electronic Industrial Revolution. The past glory of libraries, namely knowledge preserved, processed and served will now be brought to light, exploring the important aspects of complexity of phenomena of library materials convential to the users. As the old proverb goes :

'Present is the child of the Past and Father of the Future'.

The past glory of libraries is in no way inferior to the present trend. Wonderful wealth of information was stored, processed and disseminated. Constant wars, petty quarrels were the rule of those days. During such interventions, knowledge of writing, reading and recording brought a close-up to some extent with collaboration. Our modern libraries can no longer afford to look back but to aim at marching forward.

The knowledge of the past stands as a towering monument to man's skill and his desire for advancement of civilization. His craving for learning never ends and still, it intrigues the learned, the learner and the learning for more and more introspection. From time immemorial, library is considered as the Seat of Learning, collecting knowledge for the use of its readers. The use of libraries is a great boon to encourage learning and gaining of knowledge and up-lifting of education. If we analyse the Five Laws of Library Science, we perceive the high standard which is expected in every library, not only in rendering of its services to readers but also in its effective and efficient management.

The changing dimensions in academic libraries today, call not only for automated services, but also the change of their traditional role of being mere store-houses of books into effective service libraries. Radical improvements and change in the working of our libraries can be brought about by library oriented studies in the academic courses of studies. A greater use of libraries will widen the mental horizon of its users. In the modern set up of our society, the college libraries play an important role to develop the spirit of inquiry, initiative, scientific temper, linguistic skill for effective speaking, writing and so on. To create reading habits at the academic level and even among adults, it is very crucial to choose books carefully. The choice of right books helps the readers not only to enjoy their reading, but also it gives them an incentive to build home libraries and various other kinds of special libraries, later in life.

Often students' needs are taken for desires and they are controlled. The interpretation of the users' demands as needs rather than wants, moves the college libraries to change their concept of library holdings and library services. Proper use of library resources can be made useless without its proper management. The imprisonment of learning potential is to be released in libraries. Books, journals, slides and computers must be assessed and their effects later evaluated to meet the needs of the Educational System.

Libraries are above all social institutions, a teaching-learning milieu in which retrieval of information is only a part. If the new technology destroys this environment, it will also destroy what it is trying to maintain and improve. In larger libraries and those which are connected with the Educational Technologies, the need of the A.V. resources becomes vital. There is a great change in man's need for information. More than books, the emphasis of information-seeking is laid on information storage, information processing, information handling, information transfer and information retrieval. There are nations rich in information and nations weak in information. To meet these needs of information sharing even at the college level, we need a chain of Information Centres.

User Education can be defined as a programme to guide and to instruct the potential users either individually or in a group. This programme should enable the users to know their own requirements, to formulate their own needs, and to use the library information services effectively so that they may easily learn to access these services. User Education is a combined effort of the libraries and of the faculty in developing courses for study conducted in classroom. User Education is meant not only for library readers, but it is also needed to educate or further educate the Librarians to be better Agents of User Education. User Education today is a very inviting and important concept in libraries. Users are the focal point of the Library System. The aim of the library service is to serve the users, hence a motivation and an awareness has to be created in the users i.e. marketing information. Thus salesmanship becomes one of the attributes of the Librarians.

To meet the need of the modern youth in our college libraries, it is necessary to introduce Film Clubs where books on Film-making, Film direction, Film acting and Film reviews could be made available. Films, no doubt, are important mediums of social communication and education. Besides films, books also contribute a unique stimulus to the imagination. But films help to transmit an up to date variety of current facts which may at times also encourage an intellectual laziness.

Another important item to make our college libraries to be Centres of Information is the introduction to build up Oral Sections relating to current events, politics, the arts and the local histories, popular cultures, and so on. There could be an information section where students could get information relating to jobs availability and information regarding the conduct of various courses. Thus the students could make a choice for their future life while still at college studies.

The users of the library must be convinced that the continuing learning is worthwhile and that the process of education does not end with examinations. They must have confidence to be learners and to stand on their own, to possess autonomy to select and to direct their own future study experiences. Of course, this is not an easy task. It is rather a time-consuming work to capture the interest of users on this line. It becomes a real challenge for college librarians without the cooperation of the teaching staff.

A college librarian needs knowledge, skill and ability to sympathise and to understnad the needs of the users. This knowledge is not part of the professional tool-kit as a content of the professional education. A college Librarian musut be able to communicate maeaningfully in subject terms and must cultivate a deep understanding of Education itself. At the same time a Librarian is called to have a deep understanding and involvement in the needs of the students as well as that of the staff with their motivation and demands. This can be done only through a greater involvement with the classroom activities. Here lies the stimulus of the user education and other education-oriented activities. User Education does not stop with library orientation. Rather, the latter is the beginning of user education and which must be a continuity in the library. User Education co-relates with study skills and library skills.

The library staff has also to present a welcoming, comfortable and relaxed atmosphere to further the process of self-learning. Leisure reading must be encouraged to get into the process of self-learning. The library resources must involve a variety of media which can stimulate the learning process. Today we have the language learning for students who wish to go abroad. This learning is imparted through tapes and books. It can be ideal self-learning process at their free time in the college hours. Paper cut-outs could be placed on boards to satisfy the other informational needs of the users.

In some of the Western Libraries, films, video cassettes are used to illustrate the practical operations of the library, such as those showing the strength of its holdings or books available for reference. The library already described in Chapter 4 is an ideal model for any college library to start with. These techniques can be used by some of the larger college libraries. It would help the users to use the resources especially when faced with diverse and complex opinions and to weigh, consider and review them.

In some of the important Libraries in India as well as in the West, A.V. and Computer services are generated in addition to the various printed resources within the collections of the Libraries. There is no doubt, that some of this material is owned by various departments. But the multi-media potential of the college library must be accepted.

Another method to imporve user education would be that the Librarian be a source of advice on library resources available. The library must be the point of contact with the extension of its retrieval of resources with the local and national resource agencies. Links with the outside world do not increase the library resources, but they are important helps for the growth of library services.

It is not easy to convince students at the college level to continue the learning process for life-time. This may not be relevant to day-to-day living. Life and learning often at times pulls in opposite direction. To benefit from both, there is need for an inner compulsion. The starting point is WONDER, curiosity and the joy of discovery. This is the key to learning how to learn.

Years ago Anderw Carnegi remarked in his anthology :

> 'our young people often get educated for life upon some other planet than the one they live in. Today interactions between life and learning include new technological possibilities and seek more leisure. The joy of discovering aroused in the classroom or through work in libraries can be effective to meet this problem. Students must be encourged to get through knwoledge, the best out of print and non-print resources. Often many of the students loose their interest in specializing themselves once their education ends. This occurs when compulsion for studies is replaced by love of learning. It is a disease in Education which must be avoided if Education has to remain library-oriented'.

Orientation Progarmmes should cover the topics like :

Subject Bibliographies
Publishers Catalogues
Reviewing Periodicals
Book Selection sources and aids

Acquisition Policy
Classification and Cataloguing, etc.
Systems of Charging and Discharging of books to readers
Working hours of the library
Reference and information services
Reference sources and its characteristics
Documentation
Abstracting services.

Each of these topics must involve students in formal work and in thinking and not just listening. They should be stimulated to read and to investigate in the library. For practical guidance, users must be shown the shelf arrangement of book collection, the library catalogue and its use as to how to find the required document. For this we need:

- to take the students round the library to the various sections.
- to teach them how to make the best use of library resources with a view to develop interest in reading good literature.
- to give them extra-curricualr reading helps for personal growth, mental development and skill for good reading.
- to motivate them to use their skills and abilities.

User Education is the child of new technology. Melvil Dewey, the Great Librarian of the West, based his first teaching curriculum on :

- Library service function – subject discipline
- Patterns of library service
- Specialized assistance to readers.

User Education has been entitled by the Signage Research Institute as "Technical and Psychological" consideration for "Sign Systems in Libraries". **Sign Guides** is a developing theory for communication about physical arrangement of spaces in any library. Engineers are guided by signs. Traffic is guided by signs to a smooth flow of traffic. So too signs in Libraries produce effective use of resources by the users. Signs serve the users and answer their requirements. Signs convey a message from the sender to the receiver namely, from the book shelf to the reader. These signs are analysed according to various groups of users.

User Education is divided into three parts (Fig. 13.1). We could summarise it thus :

(1) Educating the users as to the use of the library
(2) Acquainting the users with the holdings of the library
(3) Familiarising the users with the tools and devices used by the library.

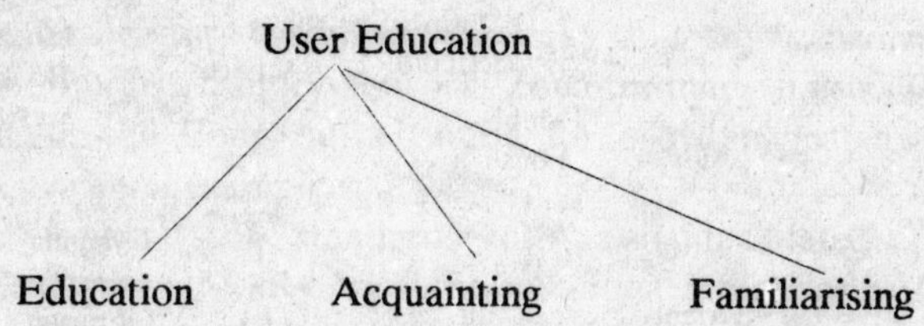

Fig. 13.1 : User Education

USER Education can be approached under two aspects (Figure 13.2):

- By library orientation courses
- By lectures on library devices, tools and collections.

These two aspects can further be divided as follows; Library Orientation courses are subject-oriented and could be divided into

(1) Guide tour round the sections
(2) Seminar organization and tutorials
(3) Tapes and Videos
(4) Exhibitions
(5) Handbook
(6) Practical exercises with lectures and preparation or Bibliographies
(7) Travelling Workshop Experiment i.e. subject-oriented programmes – information packages.
(8) Individual helps.

The lecture method could further be spelt out in the following ways :

(1) *Short-Range Services* :

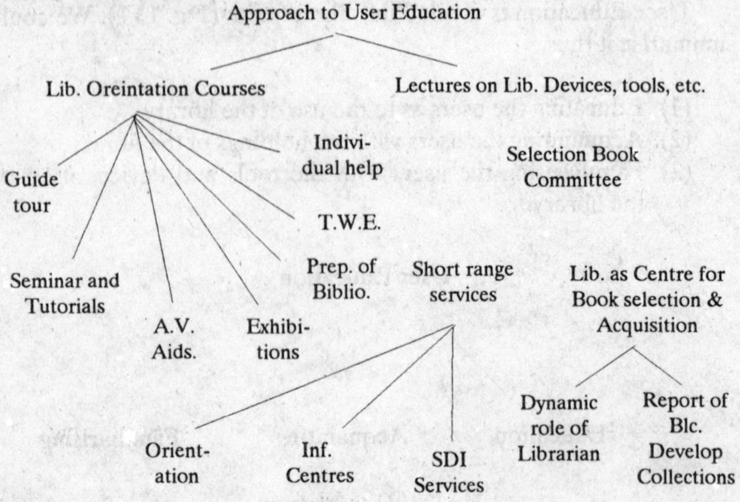

Fig. 13.2 : Approach to USer Education

- User Education Orientation
- Marketing information – three National Centres set up by the UGC at Bangalore, Baroda and S.N.D.T., Bombay.
- SDI Reprographic Services

(2) *Library Selection Book Committee* :
This Committee to be set up with students also as members to draw up Book Selection Lists.

(3) *Library to be the Centre* for Book Selection and Acquisition – Role of Libraries :
- Primary selection by the library staff with the Librarian playing a dynamic role.
- Draw up a periodical Report of the Balance development of library collections.

The components of USER Education are five :

(1) For the independent use of libraries
(2) To impart Education to Users to use the libraries effectively.
(3) To create User awareness
(4) To establish User orientation

(5) To give Bibliographical instruction to train the Users to the skills in using the libraries.

The User Education is the genuine fountain on which the Educational System needs to be re-structured. It is necessary to have a socially related Educational System. Library Orientation and Bibliographical instruction are the two areas of User Education. Bibliographical instruction is necessary to understand the User Report strategy to solve their problems. It is done through the use of:

Encyclopaedias
Biological Abstracts
Library Catalogues

Principles of study, search study and subject analyses

We could translate the User Education in the words of A.C. Woolneri as:

> "the ability to use a library is an acid test of the reality of Education.
> It is a spring of hope and winter of despair
> It is the best of times and the worst of times
> Using the library effectively is the route to intellectual treasure."

The objectives of User Education can be achieved through investigating as to what users do and do not do in libraries. User Education is an expanded orientation designed for self-help by the user and the use of all media is necessary. It helps to develop students' reference assistance for service both in and outside the library (Fig. 13.3). Sometimes students take pleasure in college studies relating to certain disciplines. There are some who never go beyond the syllabus even at a later date. Such an Education can lead not only students but even teachers and librarians who are not alert, to new discoveries, to purpose which is obscure and where disbelief reigns in life to better oneself or one's life and work.

A continuing education involves themes which are old and new and which are practical and of intellectual worth. A college library however excellent it may be, it cannot implant a desire for learning. Part of this problem is caused by lack of information-gathering skills

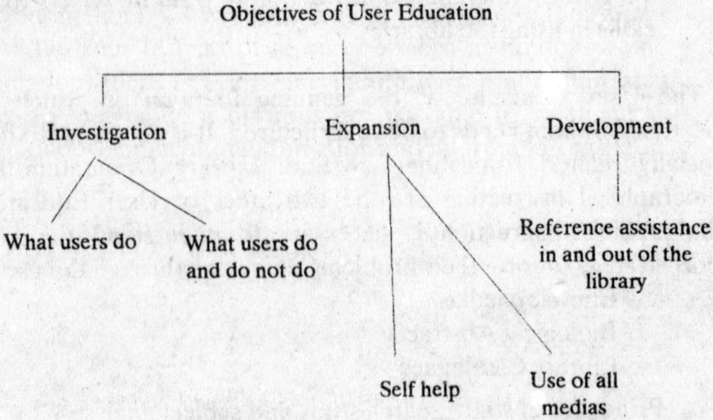

Fig. 13.3 : Objectivies of User Education

and a learning experience on the part of librarians. College libraries have therefore to be made multi-media based and to be an ideal laboratory for learning.

With the Role of Libraries, the Roele of Librarians in the modern educational system needs our attention too. Nevertheless, to the college librarians, like that of the college teachers is given a God-given Mission to make the students experience their love and compassion through their services and especially to promote this Mission by listening to them.

Classroom education today does not emphasize the student's search for the sources through reading of articles, discussions or conducting study experiments. Hence, the role of libraries has not become significant in the Educational system.

College libraries are academic and educative. This improtant factor is affected by all that the librarians and their libraries do. A college linbrarian is an Educationist. An efficient college librarian can contribute to a better educational experience for the students, Librarians perform a teaching and research role formally and informally when they assist users in their study persuits. This is really the function of any qualified librarian in the modern library system.

The academic libraries in the country have yet to gain their importance and proper place in the changed concept of modern education. The libraries form the central organ of any educational institution and, as such, the UGC Report of 1921 states:

> "a library is not only the basis of all teaching and study, but the importance of its Role is seen in research works and without the libraries, no addition to knowledge can be made".

The use of libraries is often affected by the attitude of persons who have enjoyed a good service. Such a person will quickly develop a sense of appreciation as to how a library can help them in their work. This perception in turn will affect the student-use. They even may touch on materials which perhaps are not even read by the teachers. This material can give thought-provoking opinions. Up to now, if college libraries are heavily used, it is only for the purpose of passing the examination.

Collection in a college library must be such that they are far superior to that of the classroom notes. Resource-based learning for students must be valuable in terms of variety and beneficial as an educational experience. The use of libraries should create opportunities both for teachers and students for discussing problems or opinions arising from their reading in the library. This can be as productive and as equivalent to the listening in a classroom. Such an attitude does not come merely from the tremendous educative power but from the wisdom to understand and to select the right books to read within the limited time.

At the same time, the college library service must be up to date with the needs of the classroom. Thus a C.A.S. service directing the staff to new books, new articles, educational records/cassettes, Government Publications and such other reading materials of relevance, whether the library is computerized or not, is an important ingredient to encourage staff-use.

To make the User Education effective, the libraries must work to know the special leanings of the staff members and of the students as users of the library. This can be done through informal conversation.

A large section of our society today hungers for a second learning chance as mature students. This is evident through A.E.P. The Open University and Distance Learning Educational Systems are introduced to make education available to all. Here the Role of library education becomes more vital even at the college and

University level. In such a education, the absence of class and teacher in supplemented by the libraries. The college and University libraries can be Centres to tackle such readers and make available their recorded knowledge in the library holdings.

We have many strong examples of this Adult Learning process. John Mackinnon Robertson (1856-1933), a self-educated man and an open learner, long before the concept of self-learning was even recognized, became a prolific author on Elizabethan literature, religion and economics. In his experience of using the libraries for self-learning, he remarks:

> "The achievement of a mind worth having in old age, must be the product of ALL one's proceeding years – whatever the nations of the world lack, be they rich or poor, they all have one thing in comon – too many blockheads to square mile".

Robertson found the remedy for learning in selective reading. Modern society needs the use of many other resources than books and journals to be educated. Robertson felt sorry for those young people who remained unencouraged for educating themselves and never were able to achieve the skills to become active and independent life-long learners as he was.

14

Student-view of Academic Libraries

The authoress after interviewing several students of various academic libraries, has drawn up the following evaluation of libraries in academic institutions. This evaluation is surely a means to be better librarians to work and to create better libraries and so make them better places of services to our readers. This evaluation places before us the condition of our academic libraries today as witnessed by the several types of readers. Their comments and suggestions will help to give us better insights for skilful library services. Due to the prevailing financial crisis, the condition of several of our academic libraries is rather inefficient. The readers comment that both the librarians as well as the readers help to bring the libraries to such a state.

From ancient times, libraries in India have always been looked upon as the life of the Educational System. But unfortunately this does not prove to be true today of our libraries in India. The Educational System itself being on its downward trend, the libraries are nothing less than mere storehouses of books. Needless to assert that most of our acedemic libraries are in a deplorable state with its chaotic functions. They fail to meet the needs and interests of readers who find no other way out but to go in for market notes for their study.

The very thought of some of the academic libraries, remark the readers that it brings to their minds a dimly-lit room with broken racks, filled with dust and cowebs. Libraries such as these remain closed for no reason and the readers would be lucky if they found them funtioning at any time.

In an ideal Educational System, an academic library is the Centre of academic life. Libraries being the backbone of every Educational Institution, there can be no real progress in education without them. A library can be considered as the Fountain Head from whence flow the waters of knowledge and wisdom. The busiest hours of any enthusiastic reader are spent mostly within the library. The very atmosphere of the World of Books acts as a tonic exciting the appetite of the intellect even of those readers who seem to be indifferent. Unfortunately our libraries are still far away from this ideal. Rather, they are often found ill-managed, ill-housed and ill-equipped.

Education has two components, namely—the Teacher and the Book. A good library can be a valuable support to education as much as a sound education system is dependent on good libraries. Any form of educational works without libraries becomes meaningless. Frederick J. Marsh, Chief Observation Officer, London, speaking of Indian Libraries has remarked that—

> "A Nation that allows destruction of its libraries, deserves to have its history written by its enemies" and that "without the generous support from the Government Authorities, the cry for survival of the best of libraries will go unheeded".

Such a remark should be a strong incentive for our nation to preserve our libraries which from ancient times are considered to be the Temples of Knowledge and Learning.

Seeing the importance of libraries in the context of modern Education and with the development of Research and Technology, our libraries have not yet been able to provide the youth and the citizens of the country, the Educational Facilities through the establishment of good academic libraries. To be able to move freely in a world of Books today is one of the privileges of the modern Education. A library of books itself is a University of Knowledge feeding the intellect. Variety of readers visit the libraries – some to peep into the daily newspapers, others to learn and yet others to satisfy their curiosity for knowledge through a intellectual research.

The importance of libraries is vital in an economically backward country like India. Hence without adequate library facilities, education becomes a mere myth. It is tragic that libraries are not appreciated for what they are. A well-equipped library alone could help to raise the intellectual level of not only readers but also that of the teachers in academic institutions. It is the teachers who have to enkindle among the readers the love for libraries. Libraries form the nucleus of Higher Educational System, and thus foster a deeper sense of creativity with its unlimited available resources. Readers have to be attracted to the use of the library, for its knowledge can be imbibed through a taste for reading.

Observing the fuctioning of libraries, the readers have this to say:

> 'When we look into the working of some of the libraries or rather most of them, the mis-use of funds stands prominent'.

But the proper functioning of any library also depends very much on the readers using the libraries. It becomes the responsibility of the users of the library to maintain or to create an atmosphere of peace and calm within the library and for orderliness on shelves by placing the right book in its right place and by handling every reading material with care. The many comments and criticisms given by the several readers have brought to light many of the shortcomings of our library functions. It is for the librarians to reflect on them and be aware of them.

Our libraries too lack proper study rooms with an atmosphere of silence which induces power for concentration and research. Many of the libraries being managed by untrained hands, the libraries function inefficiently. Often books which form the asset of libraries are not properly cared for. Such ill-functioned libraries become useless institutions in the System of Education. To bring our libraries to a proper functioning order, there is need to re-model the whole library system. On the other hand, the misuse of library facilities by readers is an invitation to keep the libraries locked for a long period of time. On the part of the readers too, they stand guilty for disfiguring and mutilating the important reading materials which does not help the libraries to grow in a healthy manner.

The absence of up to date catalogues makes sitill more difficult for the readers to find their required material for reference work. Often the rare manuscripts of Indian Cultural Heritage are left uncared for and the result is, that such precious documents are allowed to perish. Useful and newly purchased books on the other hand are put together and they remain unprocessed for months together. The management in many of the academic libraries is so unscientific that the condition of libraries is miserable and libraries become places of problem for serious readers.

Good books are not only good friends to the readers but they help in building up an all-round personality develoment of every reader who uses them. Such readers desire to have an up to date knowledge by consulting General Knowledge Books like the social Science Encyclopaedia and various Competitive Magazines. This type of reading material becomes an incentive for readers to visit modern libraries. A good library must be able to meet the expectations of its readers. The library should create Competitive Magazine Section where readers can prepare themselves for competitive tests and freely collect knowledge for Aptitude Tests and other General knowledge. With this type of literature, the readers would be more confident in presenting themselves for UPSC, BPSC, Banks and other Competitive Examinations.

We do lack the facility of a good library in most of our Educational Institutions. Books for higher Education are beyond the purchasing power to the readers. They therefore look up to the libraries to fulful this need for them. But sad to say, that no up to date editions are made available to the readers. Ultimately they are forced to depend on notes from tutors and cheap printed guide books for their study.

How the libraries are viewed by the readers depends very much on the efficiency of the librarians who are its managers. For the readers or users of the library, the Librarian becomes the most prominent figure, responsible for the functioning order of the library. The readers expect the librarians to be scholarly persons with a specialized training. The librarians have a key role to play in making the libraries effective agents of service. Every librarian bears the reponsibility for the smooth and efficient running of the library. Hence, every librarian who is trained to manage a library must cultivate a professinal skill, be interested in all the readers or users of the library and be willing to help them in a friendly and loving way. The readers also expect the librarians to be lovers of discipline. To have a good disciplined library is one of the basic rights of the readers and it is their privilege to demand for better library facilities. Both, the librarians as well as the readers together share the responsibility for efficiency in libraries.

It is time that the academic libraries emerged from their

deplorable situation and rejuvinated themselves as a phoenia to see the light of day. There is need for a good autonomous Administrative Body consisting of officials and enthusiastic librarians to improve the condition of our academic as well as other libraries. A Committee should also be created to supervise the functions of the working libraries from time to time. For better and quick library services computer services and other automation services must be introduced in our academic libraries. Open access to the shelves although a risky task, would give the users more freedom to choose materials of their choice with greater leisure and satisfaction. Moreover, our libraries should also work for longer hours.

All this can be visualized only in libraries where there are dedicated and trained library staff, who do need to up date themselves through an on-going education which is a life-time learning. Continuing Education is a kind of renewal of an urge for the individual to keep abreast with the chosen field of knowledge and profession. It involves an understanding of interactions with the changes taking place in every sphere of human activity. Librarians have been experiencing rapid changes in the field of librarianship due to:

(1) The changing developments in the structure of knowledge
(2) The changing perceptions of users of information
(3) The variety of information packages in print-on-paper media.

To meet these developing changes our modern libraries have to be alert and self-renewing with skills and management.

Further, it is not enough to equip our libraries with well qualified and trained librarians, nor even to equip the libraries with rich holdings, if there be no proper trained users to use the library collections. The under-utilization of available library resources is influenced by various factors, some of which are user-related while others are system-related. Ignorance of the library resources prevents a user from benefiting from the use of libraries, and the increasing of complexities also leaves the user ignorant of the resources available in libraries.

So far our libraries concentrated on library works such as acquisition, cataloguing and classification of resource materials; and the user for whom the works were performed was in the background. Often this has resulted in the non-use of processed resources. User

Education in its current form would be to lay greater stress on the users. This will bring about an achievement for better utilization of our resources and at the same time highlight the means to improve our information system.

The scope of user education has changed with the times. it begins with orientation and bibliographic instruction and it goes further to help the users to recognize their own informational needs as well as to formulate those needs. User Education leads to bridge the gap between information services and potential users. It offers instruction for effective and efficient use of libraries and information services. User Education teaches the users to acquire skills for information retrieval and to assess the library and information services insofar as, use is made of them.

The pre-requisites for user education programme would include:

(1) close cooperation between the teaching staff and informational professionals for drawing up the instructional programmes
(2) motivated instructors and students
(3) availability of sufficient resources and manpower
(4) instituttional structure to support these programmes

Programmes such as these, are likely to raise the expectations of the library users with regard to the use of library collections. A.C. Woolner has said: "Ability to use a library is an acid test of reality of the Education", and our libraries have to prove this.

The concept of User Education in USA Colleges developed out of efforts of Patricia B. Knapp of Merideith College and that of Thomas G. Kirk of Earlham College. The concept of short and long range reference service is the precursor of the new concept of USER Education. Library orientation and Bibliographic instruction form the Two Arms of User Education. The three components of User Education are:

(a) Users' Awareness of library resources
(b) Library Orientation and teaching of library skills
(c) Bibliographic instruction

All these components lay stress on educating the user. In Hempshire College in USA, the elitist institution established in 1970 the objectives of user education which could be achieved through the following three tasks:

(1) Investigate as to what the users do and do not in libraries
(2) An expanded orientation programme designed for self-help by the users utilizing all media as necessary.
(3) a progrmame to develop students reference assistance for service both in and outside of the library.

If our academic libraries are to be used efficiently in the instructional programme, librarians must not only be teachers, but teachers must be librarians.

In the library, the **user** occupies the key place. To meet the demands of the user, one has to study thoroughly what the user wants, what they think about the library and how they feel about the environment prevailing within the library.

User Education does not operate in a vacuum. It is directly related to the changing concept of Education. Needless to say that the core of professional work for librarians remains in user education. In view to give importance to user education, it would not be out of place to suggest a Centre for User Education to motivate the librarians for conducting the User Education in libraries.

A close study of our academic libraries and their functions reveal the sorry state of affairs. Often libraries are the victims of apethetic attitude of Government and other responsible authorities, in facing acute financial problems. To point out a few ills that render our academic libraries as non-profitable service institutions in the progress of Education would help our librarians to take necessary steps to better the functional works in Libraries:

(1) Libraries are not well-equipped with the needed furniture, collections and other facilites and are not spacious enough for accommodating the increasing number of readers.
(2) There are Budget dificits – hardly 1 per cent of the Education Budget is spent on libraries, when the UGC and the Commissions like the Kothari Commission have recommended 6.25 per cent of the total Education Budget to be spent on libraries. Economic and financial crisis are also the major factors for poor functioning of

our academic libraries.

(3) The reading habit among the readers is on the decline. The cause for this could be credited to – unfair means at examinations which kills the initiative for reading of tests and reference books. The A.V. media today has posed a threat to Print India and which could foster a greater interest to know more through books and which in modern times occupies an important place in the intellectual activity of the people and the users of libraries.

(4) The service conditions of librarians is very poor in many of the States in the country and librarians are treated more on par with clerical staff of pay when they have been raised to be on par with the teaching staff.

To modernize libraries today which are already in bad shape is a problem. The libraries lack proper scientific storage system and precious documents are neglected. The percentage of literacy in the country being low, a proper academic environment must be created through richer and better library system if Education has to be of National responsibility. The allotments of funds for the growth of libraries is meagre, but wonders could be worked if this meagre amount is used methodically. Mr. Shetge, the Chief Librarian at the American Centre, Bombay, has remarked –

> "Most of our libraries are under-staffed and the existing staff at least in most of the libraries perform clerical functions rather than service functions of a modern library."

15

School Libraries

The changing role of school libraries in present scenario indicated that the library being a Social Institution, is set up by the society to serve its ends. A school library is often considered as a routine requirement without recognizing its importance in learning process and in promotion of reading habit among the school children. Hence the school libraries are among the most neglected ones, when every state in the country is making efforts to develop the Educational System.

The methodology of teaching is rapidly changing too giving more stress to Vocational Education, self-study, self-learning and so on, then to classroom-oriented teaching methods. The curriculum, the teaching methods and library are the various tools that link the school with its community.

J. Leih Wilson, an eminent educationist of British India, speaking at a Conference in 1933, at Calcutta, expressed his opinion about school libraries in India, bringing out their meaning and potentialities. To quote Mr. Wilson's words:

> "A School library means for the child a new world of spiritual, cultural adventures; for the teacher an untold increase in resources and power. It means for the school a new atmosphere of learning, a new vision of intellectual things. It means, for the home, elements of common interest and the development of the habit of reading for its aesthetic value alone. It means for the Public Library, a growing clientele of

> intelligent patrons, for unless the habit of reading is inculcated in the child at school, there would be little or on demand on the part of the adult for a public library."

These few lines bring to light the great responsibility of library use at an early school-going age. B.S. Kesavan puts this very thought in a better perspective when he says:

> "A school Library is the most strategic point in an institution and it compensates for poor and bad teaching."

If we survey the school libraries today, we find that there does not seem to exist any school libraries in the context of primary and secondary educational system in India. There are more than 80 per cent of school libraries with no facilities of any kind for their growth and survival. Improvement of school libraries is of vital importance. They have a very great role to play in the Education of the students and in creating reading habits among them. To do this, these libraries require adequate funds and a well-trained staff.

Dr. S.R. Ranganathan as early as in the nineteenth century, felt and expressed that – "the result of modern re-thinking on Education is to make the library the heart of the school from which every activity in the school radiates and by which, it all gets irradiated".

It is unfortunate, that the school libraries in our country are not functioning as effective instruments of Education. Those libraries which are well equipped with the reading materials, have closed access so that school children are denied the benefits of reading books at leisure. The teachers too do not look upon the use of libraries as part of their teaching process. They impart knowledge in classrooms mainly from text-books. Very often school libraries remain and are maintained as an addition to the school building in the care of a teacher. Very few school libraries today function as a nerve centre of the teaching programme.

However, some public school libraries in the urban areas are managed by trained professionals and are well organized with a fairly good collection of over 10,000 volumes. But such libraries are very few. In these areas the library-use is made compulsory for students and classroom assignments are based on library resources. The Librarians too of such libraries are active in their mission to meet the needs of the User Education.

Aim of School Libraries

Importance of libraries in Education and its aim may be placed in the following terms:

(1) To foster interest in reading and to make the young minds be familiar with books as sources of information and leisure.
(2) To help children to become independent in finding and selecting important relevant information for their studies.
(3) To encourage a life-long Education and to create a longing for new knowledge.
(4) To make available to teachers the resoures of the library for their own professional growth.
(5) To bring out the potentials in the personalities of students.
(6) To create in them a searching mind in the use of all the library resources.

Dr. Ranganathan has laid down as a primary object of the school library, that the library should act as a lever, enabling the students through its functions and services to find out facts from the printed sources in its collections.

The Report of the Secondary Education Commission (1952-53) has recommended that:

(1) as the proper use of a well equipped school library is absolutely essential, for efficient working of Educational Institutions and for encouraging library and cultural interests in students, class and subject school libraries should be used for this purpose.
(2) Trained Librarians should be employed in Secondary school Libraries and teachers be given some training in the basic principles of library work.
(3) The school libraries should make the library facilities available to the public where there are no public libraries. All libraries, be they local or public, should have especial sections on children and adolescents.

In India we do not as yet have a network of public libraries to cater to the needs of children and the adolescents. As such, it is for the school libraries in every State to develop and to organize these sections.

A school library cannot be separated from the school educational system. The educational goals can be achieved only through a school library. The educational activities can be improved immensely with the regular use of school libraries.

An all India Educational Survey conducted by N.C.E.R.T. of school Libraries in 1987 shows that:

(1) there are 5,89,031 schools recognized and only 41.08 per cent have libraries.

(2) 17.8 per cent schools have less than 100 books
9.6 per cent schools have 100-249 books
5.3 per cent schools have 250-499 books
3.64 per cent schools have 500-999 books
2.52 per cent schools have 1000-1999 books
94 per cent schools have 2000-3999 books

(3) in all there are 1,441 full trained librarians.

This proves that the situation of school libraries is very poor even to this day. A good school library should have at least 500 books. A good school library can be a powerful force for Edcuational Excellence and help the individuals to play their role effectively in the society.

The New Education Policy has offered many challenges to improve both Education and the library facilities. But the efforts still seem to be a struggle to bring about a real development in education as well as in libraries. It is the librarian who has to face these challenges and respond to the changing needs of the society and lead forward the progress of school libraries. The ancient view that a school library is merely a room containing books and that the librarian is of having no age limit or education, 'does not hold good in this age of science and technology. The outlook on school libraries has to change with the technological development. The classroom oriented education even in schools has to make room for library centered mode of learning. It is true, that a school child learns much in the classroom. But this learning could be very much enriched through the use of library learning. For an Educational Development both formal and informal education is necessary.

A school library forms the hub of all educational activities. A library even at a school level must be used for education, information, recreation and inspiration. The use of libraries can facilitate the school students to learn and to improve their writing ability for essays and competitions. Through the use of libraries, they can also get information regarding sports, atheletic performances and festivals.

The aim of every school library is expected to build its collections to suit the modern needs of the society. Hence, it is not only to be centred round the text-books and periodicals, but it should work to extend its collections to reference books like encyclopaedias, Year books, Atlases. It should further develop its collections to include non-book materials like the maps, charts, tapes, records, films and other modern medias of communication.

An academic institution is a place where young people grow physically, intellectually and socially. In doing so, they gain self-knowledge. The modern library resouces help to fill their young minds with images, ideas and imagination, creating an awareness and curiosity to know more. A well equipped library can be a powerful stimulant to draw out the latent powers of the intellect in the youth. A school library has a major contribution towards both teaching and learning. *Bullock*, a great intellectual, once remarked that a "school library is the heart of the school resources for learning". The use of A.V. methods leads to an increase in clarity and stimulation of teaching and learning process. As a result, A.V. Aids can lead to improvement in educational process by helping the teachers to demonstrate the lesson in a particular subject.

Scope and Innovation Services in School Libraries

Our academic libraries today are getting stagnated both at the school and college level with our routine work. There is lack of dynamism on the part of the librarians, there is lack of reading habit on the part of the librarians to update their professional ability, and above all there is lack of enthusiasm and alertness to know the needs of our readers. It is true that the whole standard of our functional libraries has gone dwon due to various reasons which we shall see later. But this should not bring down our spirits as we librarians, are dedicated to our porfession. Dr. Ranganathan, our Founder and Guide has left us an example of his spirit of dedication and service in the cause of libraries. He too had to face many a struggle and suffer much TO BE A LIBRARIAN THAT HE WAS. Surely he had his moments of despair but Ranganathan believed in creativity and rose above his feelings and difficulties to hold the cause of libraries for the sake of humanity.

The Legacy left us by our Father of Library Science, Dr. S.R. Ranganathan, is the Five Laws of Library Science formulated in 1931 and which form a tribunal to anwer all opposition which we meet in the carrying out of our duties as Librarians.

It is our responsibility as Librarians, to make our libraries a place to EDUCATE every user. A Library is an Educational Laboratory where the libraries in collaboration with the classroom teaching have to extend and make learning more practical to the users. To do this, the librarians have to renew their efforts for innovative services to the readers which fall under three aspects:

(1) Dynamism of Reading Habit
(2) Scope of Innovations in School Libraries
(3) Organization of our libraries so as to invite and encourage readers/users to enjoy the use of libraries with reference to children's libraries.

Dynamism

A big problem that poses all our modern libraries today is to make our academic libraries useable to readers. With the introduction of TV programmes or the Star TV for that matter of fact, the minds of our people are captured into a Video Culture. Hence there is no inclination to read. For most of us reading has become a heavy task and it leaves the readers with a feeling of disgust as through it, they do not try to discover the real values which they are seeking for, in their lives. Movies based on books are not that enjoyable as reading the book itself.

A feedback from readers on the efforts to cultivate reading habits is often: "Why should we read books other than those pertaining to our studies"? studying the compulsory texts does in no way replace the essential reading in the shape of novels, stories, biographies or any general reading, which every human mind needs to develop one's personality and improve one's surroundings and be a healthy social being in service of the society in which God has placed us. A taste for reading habit can be compared to honey: The taste of honey can be had only by tasting it and not by hearing of its taste. So too with books. Reading is a source of entertainment and it provides information. But this is not enough. We have to **Read** in order to experience entertainment and information. To know is to have knowledge. Any reading has to be experienced and this experience collected can have a life-long effect on the person concerned. For, when we read we begin to imagine and this imagination can take us to experience the innermost feelings of the characters and then we ourselves become a part of what we read. In other words, we **Absorb** what we read.

If the reading has to be profitable, it has to be **fast.** It is said that the American President, Teddy Roosevolt, read 2 to 3 books a day. H.L. Mencken,. a great writer, was able to read 250 pages in an hour. John Stuart Mill read so fast that he could not turn the pages in keeping to the speed of reading. Some persons are able to read even 1000 words or more every minute. We find this advancement mostly among the American readers for the fact that American Education or any good Education System should enforce fast reading habit and so make people more intellectual in their way of living and working.

Evelyn Wood, an American lady who discovered a new system of Reading and Learning in 1950s has developed – **Evelyn Wood Reading Dynamics.** She says, that she was able to read 15,000 words a minute and a whole novel in 4 minutes. After the Printing Press invention, this discovery was the greatest advancement in communication. This System of Reading Dynamics is a System of study and is used to train modern readers and even business people through various types of drills and exercises and skills. The technique of reading fast helps the reader to get a taste of the book in hand and it arouses interest. In order to do this, it is necessary to have:

(a) **Concentration** – (slow reading causes distractions)

(b) **'Swift underlining Hand Notion'** – use the hand as the spacer which can come only through practice. This method is very useful in reading newspapers, magazines, novels, which is usually done at spare time which is limited for every one.

At a national Conference in 1959, the following words of Bartholini were recorded. It read thus:

> "without Books, God is silent, justice dormant, natural science at a stand, philosophy lame, letters dumb, and all things are in darkness".

And Bartholini prayed thus:

> "Please God, let us do all we can to re-instate books and reading in their proper place in our national life; so that God may be heard, and justice may be awakened, that natural science may march forward to victory and philosophy thrive. That letters may speak with the tongue of angels and darkness may give place to light."

Innovation Services

This is equally important because our libraries are service libraries and the function of such libraries is to render service which is pin-pointed and quick to its readers.

Writing about an ideal school library, I ask: What is the Place of a Library in a School? We all know that a library is the Heart of the school and that it sends out stimulaing currents and that a library is the HUB of the wheel of Education – A library is an open House where readers can browse through books for information, for pleasure and for inspiration. But are our libraries working in this way? With the increase of students, it is not possible to attend to all their needs in the library. It is here that the school curriculum should allot a period or two for library work. Education is not and should not be dependent on Psychology alone. A truly Creative Education is based on the capacity of the youth for self-education, self-direction and creative work. These creative impulses in the youth are caused by curiosity and they need to be strengthened through the use of the libraries.

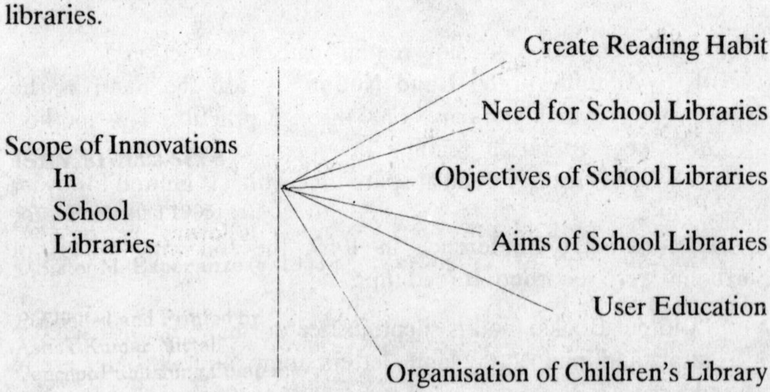

FIG. 15.1 : Scope of Innovations in School Libraries

The parents of school children too have a great role to play in the development of the personality of their children and in inculcating reading habits and in teaching them to handle books with care. This is a big Question Mark in the modern civilization.

The aim of school libraries is to advance these objectives of the parent institution and to develop reading interests (which have already been dealt with) and to discriminate users through right judgement.

The library can become a force for Education Excellence when it becomes the main link between the school authorities, teachers and the readers. The library is the **source centre** of learning for all. A school without a well-equipped library is like a Castle without an armour. It is not only collections but its function it is, that makes it a good library with its efficient services. We witness today, that due to too much teaching, too much stress is placed on completion of courses so much so that there is too little of real learning. This gives rise to very little motivation for the use of libraries.

There are 7 aims of a school library. These could be summarised as:

To inculcate reading habit
To train youth in the art of self-education
To supplement classroom knowledge
To help developoing useful hobbies through right use of libraries
To learn to co-ordinate classroom work with library work
To impart social training through library services.

Dr. Ranganathan says that "Librarianship is a noble profession. A librarian derives his or her joy seeing the joy in the faces of readers who are helped to find the right book at the right time." The Laws of Library Science are the guiding principles for every librarian to put the users in touch with the library reading materials, and to devise means and methods to invite the users through User Education to the knowledge of the library collections.

User Education is **to educate, to acquaint** and **to familiarise** the users with the library materials. This education relates to:

Orientation

Which is done through videos, handbooks, exhibitions, library tours and individual help. We can also adopt other steps to help the users for a better use of the library, such as; talks, bulletins, classification schemes, library-centred teaching in the classroom.

The value or the need of User Education is to impart education to users so that the library be used independently and effectively. User Education creates User Awareness and user skills in the use of the library materials.

Today the scope of knowledge has grown extensively and it cannot be covered up within the walls of the classroom. These boundaries of knowledge can be reached only through the use of libraries.

To organise a school library one needs a good knowledge of psychology. Every school library should organize a **children's section** so that this section serves like another house where children can move in and out of it freely and, freely choose a way to spend their time there. In the children's section books must be arranged according to the needs of various age grpups. Every child likes to gather facts and information on a variety of subjects or ideas with his or her own efforts. Hence the collection of children's section would include:

Toys and games
Books with illustrations
Descriptive, illustrative and informative books
Other general pictorial books

Young children are full of movement for seeking ideas and it is for children like these, that our school libraries could devise a modern method of learning. Story-telling or music-listening is yet another method of learning for a child and many more methods could be thought of to suit the needs of a child's mental health. TV programmes help to create curiosity in children. Movies on various religious festivals, social customs, and so on, help them to understand one another and increases their national spirit, and builds them up into one nation as they grow up.

In the organization of a school library much dynamism and imagiantion is needed on the part of the Librarian. Kumud Behn Joshi in her book entitled, 'Conteporary Approach to school library', states that the one place which is considered of utmost importance in shaping the future of mankind in its early stage is the **School Library** where one acquires knowledge through one's own efforts.

Compared to the importance given to children's libraries in foreign countries, India is not far in giving the same importance to them in the country. Much has been done to educate the rural children through a number of Literacy Camps being organized through educational institutions and individual groups, although the process in slow.

"The best way to make children good is to make them happy"—says Escar Wilde and what better and lasting thing can there be than to instil in children a love for reading.

The Need and Use of A.V. Aids

The use of A.V. aids increases learning effectiveness. A school-going child through the A.V. aids can retain 10 per cent of information which is read and 20 per cent of what is heard and 30 per cent of what is seen. A child remembers 50 per cent of what is heard and seen and then enters into a discussion. The A.V. methods can also reduce the required learning time by 40 per cent and increase retention of information by 20 per cent. These studies are an important outcome of A.V. techniques.

The advantages of A.V. methods in teaching too are quite enriching. It helps the teachers in a variety of ways:

(1) Use of prepared A.V. aids can reduce time-lost in writing on black boards, dictating notes in class.
(2) Lessons transferred into A.V. form are more stimulating and can be repeated several times.
(3) Information can be presented in a more interesting way. Thus, learning based on human voice and printed media is limited.
(4) Through A.V. aids, lessons can be prepared to meet the needs of particular groups in a classroom.
(5) Teaching can be done in specialized areas according to the requirement and dependance on written or printed resources is lessened.
(6) A.V. aids help to widen the range of information which cannot be given in detail in a classroom, like for example, information of systems, ideas, people, events, situations and so on.
(7) Knowledge gained through A.V. methods helps the teachers

as well as students to participate effectively in seminars, meetings, symposia and conferences.

(8) A.V. aids increase job satisfaction for a teacher who thus equips herself with more knowledge in her subject. Hence, the teachers are thus able to create enthusiasm and interest in any particaular subject.

(9) A.V. programmes can be duplicated for use in several places.

Due to physical format, A.V. materials form a different species of library collections. It requires additional skill in the organization of its tools, in handling and in retrievel of information through A.V. materials.

In order to be able to work a school library efficiently, the following elements need to be given due importance:

(1) A Library Committee

A library policy must be drawn up with the help of the committee for its working. In this committee there should be a student of a senior class included as the student representative.

(2) Finance

Finance is necessary for the improvement and development of school libraries. As yet, our school libraries are not yet recognised. Promotion of a good library service is dependent on finance. The Kothari Commission (1961-66) recommends the development of Book Banks in Secondary Schools and this requires the allocation of funds.

(3) Book Collection

A school library must acquire selective educational books, approved encyclopaedia, dictionaries, newspapers, periodicals, to suit the use of students; reference books, informative literature, inspirational and recreational reading, literature for vocational guidance; books for retarded readers, nation-building and character-building should add to the collections.

(4) Library Services

At least once a week there should be a library hour for each class.

Dr. Ranganathan says that this hour should be an hour of great tension and individual attention. In order to instil a proper use of libraries, the students should be given short orientation courses or talks which include topics like:

(1) Mode of handling a book
(2) Knowledge of the parts of the book
(3) Use of reference books
(4) Knowledge of classification system used
(5) Use of catalogues
(6) Use of periodicals

(5) Staff Pattern

The Recommendation of the Secondary Education Commission (1952-53) recommends a full-time trained librarian for school libraries. This is the first and the most important requirement in a school library. The librarian must posses knowledge of the basic library techniques and also technical qualifications, a sense of humour, knowledge of child psychology and a good personality. A librarian must be one who can influence the young minds and reflect the library as an essential part of education.

A school library being a service library, its documents have to be organized in a way that will attract the students by:

- Book Exhibitions
- Display of Book jackets
- Display of Newspaper clippings
- Display of a List of new arrivals
- Organize book talks, story hours for small children, quiz time, etc.

Finally, the improtance and effectiveness of a school library consists in shaping the future of individuals during their formative years of life. It is in the library that one learns to inculcate the reading habit and of acquiring knowledge through one's own efforts.

16

Epilogue

Turning back to the Library Trends, new trends have been showing themselves in large libraries, like INSDOC, DRTC and the modern State Libraries. Many of the Public Libraries as well as the academic libraries have been using the automated services in the work of Circulation and On-Line Cataloguing and Bibliographic services. Recently, provision has been made for more than 50 major libraries of various scientific institutions, Research Laboratories, Medical Colleges and Universities in Calcutta to the brought under a computer network CALIBNET for mutual sharing of information. This is indeed a mojor break-through in information technology.

This project has also been taken up by the Information Centre – NISSAT. In spite of the impetus given by Dr. S.R. Ranganathan for the development of computerization in information storage and retrieval system, our country is still far behind in the development of a proper and systematic library system.

The modern trends in the use of computers, xeroxing, Audio Visual Aids and other electronic devices, help in speeding up the library services to the users. A lot of reading material could be preserved with these devices and made available to the users when needed. At the same time, these devices would also help in avoiding backlags and thus bring about a better uniformity and a greater efficiency in the works of the library functions. On the other hand, these devices would also serve as time-saving devices for the library staff, so that, they would get more time to guide the users in the right use of the library materials.

The historical background of libraries reveal the uneven development of Public Library System in the State of Bihar. The development of the Public Library system does not seem to have gone very much beyond the blue print of the First Five Year plan.

The various political circles and the endless disturbances in the improvement of the Educational System, have made a great impact not only on Education, but also on library services. There seems to be a lack of institutional pressure groups to impress on the State Government the need to fund the Library System in the State of Bihar as well as in many other States in the country where the Library Legislation is not yet enacted.

To improve the Librar' Movement, the Government of Bihar has created a State Library Planning Committee through the inspiration of Raja Rammohun Roy Library Foundation Scheme. This Committee consisting of eleven members is set up under the Chairmanship of the Minister of Education, Bihar. The other official members to help with the work of the Committee are:

- The Education Commissioner
- The Director of Higher Education
- Director, Raja Rammohun Roy Library Foundation
- The Joint Secretary of Education
- The President of the Bihar Rajya Pustakalaya Sangh
- Librarian, Bihar State Central Library
- Superintendent of Libraries, Education Department, Bihar.

and a few other eminent persons in the Library Profession.

Further, the function of the State Library Planning Committee could be analysed as follows:

(a) To ensure regular payment of State contribution and sanction of regular matching grants to the Raja Rammohun Roy Library Foundation.

(b) To scrutinize and recommend proposals for assistance to the Raja Rammohun Roy Library Foundation.

(c) To select books and other reading materials for the State District Central Public Libraries, Divisional Public Libraries, District Public Libraries, Sub-Divisional Public Libraries, Block Public Libraries, Village Public Libraries and special Public Libraries, according to the needs of each reading community and in conformity with the guidelines laid down by the Raja Rammohun Roy Library Foundation.

(d) To select the names of the Public Libraries which need to be assisted by the Raja Rammohun Roy Foundation.

(e) To distribute books and other reading materials to the selected Public Libraries.

(f) To plan out other library activities to bring about the development of the public Library Movement in the State of Bihar.

The public library system would function effectively if facilities were created for libraries to be centres of attention towards the neo-literates through the use of Audio Visual aids and popular magazines. These technological modes would help to promote not only literacy programmes but also to motivate readily the reading habits in general.

A better funding of the Public Library System on the other hand would be a way to support the Edcuational System in aiming at the Higher Education Standard of Learning in the country, Shortage of funds cripples libraries, their functions and their service to the public. For a better organization of librarires and in order to normalize the staffing pattern having proper uniformity of grades of pay scales and suitable working conditions in libraries, there is a vital need for the enactment of the Library Act in all the States of the country.

If the potential of the Public Library System is to be tapped, it has to be tied up with the Adult Education Programme especially till such time as the latter creates an infra-structure of its own. Today we seem to be caught up within the Educational System which is facing several problems. This state of things has defeated the very existence of our academic and university libraries.

The use of libraries is no waste of time nor is it a waste of knowledge – rather, libraries help to expand knowledge and put its readers on the right track in solving their problems in various spheres of life. There is need of political will to improve and to develop our Public and Academic library situation in India which includes even the school libraries which are most neglected in the system of education. There is also need of help from our Legislators to help in the growth of library movement in the country. Libraries are for all and for the betterment of all. There can be no social change without thought-provoking information which can be found only in libraries.

The academic libraries are often looked upon as a supplementary adjuncts to educational institutions. The college and University libraries are to be looked upon and accepted as the integral part of the Educational System. With all the efforts for the growth of Library Development in our country, college libraries remain with the problem of the lack of space, lack of funds and lack of well-equipped staff. In the absence of all these factors, the Librarians are not able to do their best, neither to command respect and organize the library holdings for its proper use among the users of the library.

The greatest problem of 1990s is that, education itself seems to have become irrelevant to the needs of the society. The college and University libraries are caught up with this irrelevance as being part of the larger Educational System.

There is today need to go through radical changes of the times, and to meet them with greater spirit of confidence to go ahead overcoming all obstacles. This can be a reality only through a sincere cooperation and devoted services of the librarians in the interest of the users. To bring this change of action, there is need for automation in our libraries, and willingness to change and effectiveness in service, if our academic libraries are to march forward in the 21st century with an aim to meet the challenging possibilities of late 1990s, thus bringing about a hope for a brighter future in the cause of Higher Education in the country.

Bibliography

A Working Document, A Venkatappaiah, Workshop of 1989.

A.V. materials in academic libraries, Seminar papers – AIACME, 1986.

Administration and Organisation of College Libraries in India, G.L. Trehan, 1969, p.33.

Advances in Library and Information Science, D.C. Ojha and C.D. Sharma, V.1. 1988.

American Film Society since 1945, Leonard Quart and Albert Austen, 1984.

Application of Computer and Communication Technology, D.K.Bandyopadhyay, 1986.

Bihar, Ram Chandra Prasad, 1983, pp.204-205.

Carnegie Anthology, M.B.A. Wilson, New York, 1915 (Pvt. Pub.).

College Librarianship, A. Rennie Mc. Elroy, 'Objectives' and 'Practices', 1984, pp.12-27; 28-44.

College Libraries in India : A Survey Report, Girija Kumar, 1979. 53. *I.L.A. Bulletin*, V.XIX, N.4, 1984.

College Libraries in India, I.L.A. Seminar Papers, 1988.

Commonwealth University Year Book, S. Mathai, 1970, p.1032.

Computerization of Indian Libraries, P.S.G. Kumar, 1987, p.xxi.

Continuing Education for Librarians, ILA Seminar papers, 1984, pp.38ff; 127-130; 136ff.

Developing Horizons in Library and Information Science, C.D. Sharma and Kailash Vyas, V.II, 1983, pp.209-218.

Developing Horizons in Library and Information Science, C.D. Sharma and Kailash Vyas, V.I, 1983, pp.95-110.

Education and Income Generation for Women : Non-informal Approaches, Jessie B. Tellis, Nayak, I.S.I., 1982.

Education and Training of Information Users : An overview, T.S., Rajagopalan, 1978.

Education for Librarianship, Peter G. New, 1978, pp.142-150.

Education, Library and Information Services : Assessment and Effectiveness, ILA Seminar papers, 1989, pp. 419-421.

Elements of Demography, V.C. Sinha and E. Zacharia, 1986.

Encylopaedia of Library and Information Science, A.L.A., Chicago, 1980, p.315.

Financial Records of Public Libraries, Accounts Deptt., Education Deptt. Govt. of Bihar, Patna, 1989.

Focus of Adult Education, *Yojana*, V.32, N.11, 1988.

Growth of Libraries in India : Review, Khurshid Anis, No.4, 1972.

Handbook of Libraries Archieves and Information Centres in India, B.M. Gupta, V.1, 1984-85, pp.92-104.

Handbook of Libraries, Archieves and Information Centre in India, B.M.Gupta & Others, V.2, 1986, pp.619-627.

Handbook of Libraries, Archieves and Information Centres in India, V.5, 1987.

Handbook of Libraries, Archieves and Information Centres in India, V.1, 1984-85, B.M.Gupta and Others, pp.295-300.

Handbook of Libraries, Archives and Information Centres in India, B.M. Gupta, *et al.*, V.2, 1986.

Handbook of Libraries, Arhieves and Information Centres in India, V.1, 1984-85, pp.81-91.

Herald of Library Science, V.22, N.1-2, 1983, pp.42-45.

Herald of Library Science, V.24, N.3, 1985.

Herald of Library Science, V.25, N.1-2, 1986, pp.46-57.

Herald of Library Science, V.25, N.3-4, 1986, pp.189-194.

Herald of Library Science, V.25, N.3-4, 1986, pp.195-196.

Herald of Library Science, V.27, N.1-2, 1988, pp.62-69.

Herald of Library Science, V.27, N.3-4, 1988, pp.224-229.

I.L.A. Bulletin, V.XIX, N.1-3, 1983, pp.53-58.

I.L.A. Bulletin, V.XXIII, N.1-2, 1987.

India : Reference Annual, Ministry of Information and Broadcasting, 1979, p.48.

India's population problems, S.N. Agarwal, 3rd. rev.ed., 1989.

India, Education (Ministry of-), *Report of Advisory Committee for Libraries*, Delhi, 1958, 1961, p.31.

Indian Academic Libraries and Dr. S.R. Ranganathan : A critical study, R.N. Sharma, 1986.

Indian Academic Libraries and Dr. S.R. Ranganathan : A critical study, R.N. Sharma, 1986, pp.174-179; 226-241.

Indian Journal of Information, Library and Society, (IJILIS), A Qly. Research Journal, B.B. Shukla, V.3, N.1-2, 1990, Cuttack.

Information Technology (AIACHE Seminar), 1986.

Information Technology in Library Development – a paper presented at the Workshop, April, 1993, U.M. Thakur.

Innovation in School Libraries -- a talk delivered to experienced librarians of India, M. Esperanza, A.C., 1992.

Libraries in 21st century (AIACHE Seminar), 1986.

Libraries, Archieves and Information Centres in India, B.M. Gupta & Others, a handbook, V5, 1987.

Library Automation : Experience, methodology and technology of the library as an information system, : Edward M., Heiliger and Paul B. Hinderson, New York, 1984.

Library Technical Service : Operations and Management, Irene P. Godden, New York, pp.43-49, 1984.

Literary Studies, A. Burgess, 1968.

Marketing of Library and Information Services in India, Seminar papers, IASLIC, Calcutta, 1988, pp. 68-72.

Modernization in Libraries, ILA Seminar papers, 1988.

Nadezhda K. Krupskaya and Library Development in USSR, Cicily Kodiyan, 1989, pp.2-3, 35-49.

National and Public Libraries in India, S.P.Agrawal & Others, *(International Library Reivew)*, 1985, pp.17, 293-312.

National Education Policy, J.P. Naik, 1947-78, p.71.

New Frontiers of Education, Periodical, N.8, 1978, p.22.

Notes (AIACHE Seminar), 1986.

Planning for National Information System in India, ILA Seminar Papers, 1982.

Public Library Manifesto, UNESCO, 1949.

Public Library System in A.P., V. Venkatappaiah, 1982, p.6.

Public Relations for Libraries, Angoff, Allen, London, V.II, 1976.

Quality in Libraries, I.L.A. Conference Papers, 1986.

Ranganathan's Philosophy : *Assessment, impact and relevance*, T.S. Rajagopalan, 1986.

Reading the Screen : Introduction to Film Studies, Izod John, 1084.

Report of College and University Libraries, U.G.C. (India), 1965.

Report on Public Libraries, Office of Supdt. of Libraries, Govt. of Bihar, Patna, 1989.

School and College Libraries, S.R. Ranganathan, 1942.

Sociology of school library, S.R. Ranganathan, *Educational Review*, May, 1962, pp.97-99.

Survey Report of Public Libraries, Records of 1989.

Technological Development in Information Transfer : Some implications for academic libraries, 1982, pp.235-246 by J.F. Stirling.

The Pioneer, Newspaper, April 9, 1993, p.5.

The Public Library : Origin, Purpose, Significance, W.J. Murison, 3rd.ed., 1971.

The Statement, March 13, 1989, (Clipping).

Times of India, Local Thursday Newspaper – 'Campus Corner', April-June, 1989.

Times of India, No.20, 1968.

TOFEL (Test of English as a Foreign Language), Aoger B. Goodman and William Ince.

Training the students about the use of libraries : Whose Responsibility, Sandhu, Sarbjit Singh, '*Indian Librarian*', 1980.

What to read, J.M. Robertson, 1906.

Index

CICIL-16 Documentation Encyclopaedia of UNESCO and Education
J.C. Aggarwal and **S.P. Agrawal** Rs. 800 (set of 2 parts)

CICIL-17 Attitude Towards Information: A Study of Post-Graduate Teachers and Researchers in Social Sciences
N.G. Satish (in press)

CICIL-18 Librarianship and Bureaucratic Organisation: A Study in the Sociology of Library Profession in India
P.K. Jayaswal Rs. 175

CICIL-19 Literature Search
K.A. Isaac Rs. 150

CICIL-20 Child Education in India: Index to Scholarly Writings in Indian Educational Journals and Newspapers since independence
S.P. Agrawal and **Naresh Kanta** Rs. 100

CICIL-21 Lok Sabha and Vidhan Sabha Elections in India 1989 & 1990: Process and Results with Comparative Study of Manifestos
S.P. Agrawal and **J.C. Aggarwal** Rs. 250

CICIL-22 Islamic Studieş in India: A Survey of Human, Institutional and Documentary Sources
Mohamed Taher Rs. 180

CICIL-23 Panchayati Raj: An Annotated Bibliography
N.B. Inamdar, N.G. Satish and **Anil Takalkar** 290

CICIL-24 Information India 1989-90: Global View
S.P. Agrawal and **J.C. Aggarwal** Rs. 500

CICIL-25 First Handbook of Psychological and Social Instruments
Udai Pareek and **T. Venkateswara Rao** Rs. 500

CICIL-26 Educational and Social Uplift of Backward Classes: At What Cost and How? Mandal Commission and After
S.P. Agrawal and **J.C. Aggarwal** Rs. 275

CICIL-27 Mass Media and New Horizons: Impact of TV & Video an Urban Milieu
H.R. Trivedi Rs. 180

CICIL-28 Indian Writings on Education : An Indicator to Indian Educational Journals Grouped by Subject Deseriptors 1979 to 1986 (in two parts)
S.P. Agarwal Rs. 900 (per set)

CICIL-29 Nation in Crisis
S.P. Agrawal and **J.C. Aggarwal** Rs. 200

CICIL-30 Information India 1990-91: Global View
S.P. Agrawal and **J.C. Aggarwal** Rs. 500

CICIL-31 Development of University Libraries in India after Independence
O.P. Gupta Rs. 270

CICIL-32 Handbook on Child : With Historical Background
Pramila Pandit Barooah Rs. 320

CICIL-33 Weaker Section in Indian Society : Undiscovered Past, Uncertain Present and Unpredictable Future : Index to Writings in

Indian Scholarly Journals and 10 National Newspapers Classified under 1500 Descriptors 1886-1990
S.P. Agrawal and **Rajeev Kumar Sharma** Rs. 600

CICIL-34 Communication Informatics and Librarianship in India : An Introductory Guide to Publications Based on a Survey of Libraries in Capital City of India
S.P. Agrawal and **Pushpa Rani Sharma** Rs. 720

CICIL-35 Problems of Collection Development in Special Libraries
M.S. Sridhar Rs. 225

CICIL-36 National Information Resources for Social Sciences in India : Mobilisation, Dispersal and International Enhancement
S.P. Agrawal Rs. 225

CICIL-37 Modern History of Punjab : A Look Back into Ancient Peaceful Punjab Focusing Confrontation and Failures Leading to Present Punjab Problem, and a Peep Ahead : Relevant Select Documents
J.C. Aggarwal and **S.P. Agrawal** Rs. 400

CICIL-38 India Information Sources : Economics and Business
Kyllikki Ruokonen and Manohar Lal Rs.

CICIL-39 Educational Planning in India : With a Slant to Educational Financing and Administration, Vol. 1, Reports of Committees and Commissions, Five Year Plans, Statistical Tables
J.C. Aggarwal and **S.P. Agrawal** Rs. 650

CICIL-40 Integrated Library System : Two Case Studies : Latin America and India
Maria Luiza Rigo Pasquarelli, Rosaly Favero Krzyanowski, Ines Maria M. Imperatriz and **S.P. Agrawal** Rs. 160

CICIL-41 Social Science Information in India: Effort towards Bibliographical Control
S.D. Vyas Rs. 300

CICIL-42 Higher Education in India Since Independence: U.G.C. and Its Approach
O.P. Gupta Rs. 360

CICIL-43 Government and Politics in India: A Bibliographical Study of Contemporary Scenario Chronicling Rajiv Gandhi Era
S.P. Agrawal and **Rajeev Kumar Sharma** Rs. 500

CICIL-44 Second Handbook of Psychological and Social Instruments
D.M. Pestonjee Rs. 300

CICIL-45 Development/Digression Diary of India; 3D Companion Volume to Information India: 1990-91
S.P. Agrawal Rs. 200

CICIL-46 Development/Digression Diary of India; 3D Companion Volume to Information India: 1991-92
S.P. Agrawal Rs. 300

CICIL-47 Information India 1991-92: Global View
S.P. Agrawal and **J.C. Aggarwal** Rs. 500

CICIL-48 Committees and Commissions in India 1974, A Concept's Project, Compiled by a team of professionals guided by Virender Kumar (Vol. 12) Rs. 450

CICIL-49 Committees and Commissions in India 1975, A Concept's Project, Compiled by a team of professionals guided by Virender Kumar (Vol. 13) Rs. 450

CICIL-50 Committees and Commissions in India 1976, A Concept's Project, Compiled by a team of professionals guided Virender Kumar (Vol. 14) Rs. 450

CICIL-51 Committees and Commissions in India 1977, A Concept's Project, Compiled by a team of professionals guided by Virender Kumar (Vol. 15) (in four parts) Rs. 450 each

CICIL-52 Committees and Commissions in India 1978, A Concept's Project, Compiled by a team of professionals guided by Virender Kumar (Vol. 16) (in two parts) Rs. 450 each

CICIL-53 Subject Guide to Communication, Informatics and Librarianship in India (Based on a Survey of Library Holdings in Capital City of India)
S.P. Agrawal and **Pushpa Rani Sharma** Rs. 400

CICIL-54 Restructurring of Library and Information Science Curriculum
A. Tejomurty Rs. 250

CICIL-55 Committees and Commissions in India 1979, A Concept's Project, Compiled by a team of professionals guided by Virender Kumar (Vol. 17) (in two parts) Rs. 450 each

CICIL-56 Committees and Commissions in India 1980, A Concept's Project, Compiled by a team of professionals guided by Virender Kumar (Vol. 18) (in two parts) Rs. 450 each

CICIL-57 Third Historical Survey of Educational Development in India
S.P. Agrawal and **J.C. Aggarwal** Rs. 700

CICIL-58 Model Library Legislation
Velaga Venkatappaiah Rs. 400

CICIL-59 Indian Library and Information Science Literature (1990-91)
Sewa Singh Rs. 525

CICIL-60 Librarianship and Library Science in India
Mohamed Taher and **Donald Gordon Davis, Jr.** Rs. 350

CICIL-61 Comprehensive Glossary for Library & Information Science by **O.P. Gupta** Rs.300

CICIL-62 Information India : 1992-93: Global View by **S.P. Agarwal** and **J.C. Aggarwal** Rs. 500

CICIL-63 Automation Libraries and Reference Centres: With dBase III Plus by **R K Shula** Rs 250

CICIL-64 Modern History of Jammu and Kashmir by **J.C. Aggarwal** and **S.P. Agrawal** Rs 1200

CICIL-65 Library and Information Science by **Sister M. Esperanza, A.C.** Rs 250